NOBODY Important
Just A RENEGADE
COP

Just Me

Merv

MERVIN KOROLEK

◆ FriesenPress

One Printers Way
Altona, MB R0G 0B0
Canada

www.friesenpress.com

ISBN
978-1-03-914140-7 (Hardcover)
978-1-03-914139-1 (Paperback)
978-1-03-914141-4 (eBook)

1. BIOGRAPHY & AUTOBIOGRAPHY, LAW ENFORCEMENT

Distributed to the trade by The Ingram Book Company

NOBODY Important Just A RENEGADE COP

ACKNOWLEDGEMENTS

I want to very, very much thank my spiritual friend, Trish JARVIS, who was so gracious in undertaking the lengthy task of reading and correcting my grammar and numerous words omitted in writing this story, not once but twice. She found the time in her busy daily schedule and between looking after her young daughter and son, so this was a big task. Some cop humour stayed in the storyline, as it is from a cop's point of view. I am not by any means an author or story-teller. Some of us are just warped !!!!!!!

PREFACE

The title to this story is really the reflection of an ordinary common person who grew up in poor humble beginnings on the Canadian Prairies, who became disenchanted with his dismal life, and ran away from home and headed west. It was no different than a lot of other youths who leave home for some adventure. This adventure turned out to be an interesting, a colourful eventful career in the RCMP, with some exciting events, working undercover in the drug underworld, hanging out with prostitutes, and killers who were murderers, introduction to some celebrities, politicians, surviving a real gunfight, and eventually meeting his second wife, and embarking on several exotic vacations to different parts of the globe.

There is nothing all that important about the author, hence the title. Everybody, who has lived for a period of time has a story. It's just some stories are more interesting than others. You never know who you'll meet some day, and find out who they have met, and what those people have become. I often say to my friends that " I AM A POOR FARM BOY FROM SASKATCHEWAN ". This is my story.

Chapter 1

ARRIVING IN A SONIC BOOM

I began my life on earth on October 13th or 14th, 1947, depending on which records are to be considered. An astrological sign of LIBRA (scales of justice), which greatly governed my life from here forward. I only discovered this when I had to settle my late father's estate in 1996 while going through his records which he kept in a locked box in my parent's bedroom. In the box I found a hospital record, and a baptism certificate with my date of birth as October 13th. But my birth certificate indicates October 14th as my date of birth. My mother always said that I was born on the thirteenth. She ought to know-she was my mother. You do not often see number thirteen in a high-rise building elevator. This date came into dispute when I applied to join the RCMP. Perhaps back in 1947 the number thirteen somehow may have been viewed as a bad luck number, or at the time I entered into this world was around midnight, and the new day of October 14th, hence my official DOB.

I will always remember October 14, 1947 as a very significant date, as it was the same day that a USA fighter jet test pilot, by the name of Captain Chuck YEAGER flew faster than the speed of sound, and created the first sonic boom.

However, in checking the calendar, October 13, 1947, was on Monday, Thanksgiving Day in Canada. So, was I a Thanksgiving Day baby, Lord only knows? I have celebrated many of my birthdays on Thanksgiving Day. October 14, 1947 was Tuesday, the day of the New Moon. Big deal!!!!! Ironic as it seems, but years later these days had some significance, as my father died on October 13, 1996, and my mother died on October 14, 2014.

My earliest recollection of life was when I must have been around two and half, or three years old, and I was crying, and walking around on a partly dirt floor in a one room log house. That was our family home on the Saskatchewan prairie (a bit of a rough living with no indoor plumbing or electricity) that I shared with my parents, my older brother Chris, and my older sister, Carolyn Anne. That log house was located on a little hill next to a bluff of Saskatoon berry trees that led down to a very small valley with a creek running through it. A beaver lived there as well, as I recall a beaver dam that held the water back, and the neighbours were not getting their share. On an occasion my dad would break it open a bit to let the water run, as it was flooding some of our pastureland. There was a wood burning stove that heated the house on those cold wintery days, and where my mother did the cooking. I do not recall of ever getting burnt during my early curiosity in exploring things around this little house, but I am sure it was one quick easy lesson, and I avoided the hot stove.

My next recollection of life was that of playing outside this log house with Carolyn, who was one and half years my senior. She was always so gentle, and attentive towards me. I loved her for all her caring of me. She was my angel. We only had a few toys which we kids shared, and I do not recall any rivalry in the process. I do recall that we had a little steel toy tractor which was a model of that real version of the Massey Harris Model 44. We made do with empty cans and played in the dirt outside the house during those hot summer months.

Sometime later we moved into a small wood frame house a short distance from the log house. It also had no indoor plumbing or electricity. My parents continued working the farm, etc. I continued playing around in the dirt outside the house during those warm summer days. I remember digging deep into the soil and to my surprise a lizard came out. I got frightened of it. I guess I was told these were bad creatures, and to this day I do not feel comfortable in the presence of reptiles.

Our family household had rough beginnings with a dirt cellar below the house, which was used to store potatoes, and other provisions for the winter. The source of light was a kerosene lamp. It was the same in a lot of the farming households during that time. There were many "outhouse" (outdoor toilets) stories that humoured a lot of the community, especially in our closest town of Theodore during Halloween Day. One unlucky guy got stuck in one when he went to use his "outhouse" during the early evening. Some local bad boys snuck up on him and pushed it over with the door side facing the ground. He had a difficult time getting out.

Our water supply came from a well near the creek that ran below our house. I learned later that our parents had to fetch buckets of water for our household use. My mother would heat the water in a metal container that we called a boiler, on the wood stove. She would bathe all three of us (one at the time) in the same water. She kept us clean.

Chapter 2

THE DEATH OF MY ANGEL

My next recollection of my childhood was watching my sister, CAROLYN, who I refer to as my angel having constant nose bleeds. My parents would run around in a panic trying to do whatever to stop the bleeding. She seemed to lose a lot of blood, but through it all, she bounced back, and continued being that caring person towards me.

One other dramatic event in my young life was going over to my father's parent's house for a big family dinner, which on the Prairies was considered around twelve o'clock noon. After dinner I was playing a game of hide and seek with my cousin, Janet GARA. I hid behind the front door of the house, and stuck my left little finger between the door, and the door frame. Well, my brain did not have too much intelligence at the time, and what came next was a rude awakening, and reminder of that time which is with me to this very day. Janet opened the door and snapped the end of my little finger. Well, you can imagine my screaming and the assembly of the grandparents, other family members, and my parents milling around in a somewhat of a panic, not knowing what to do. I was soon put into my granddad's 1950 Plymouth, (what a car) accompanied by one of my dad's sisters, with my granddad driving, and off we went speeding to Theodore Hospital. I am not sure what happened next, but I was mended up, and to this day, my left little finger is shorter than my right little finger.

Well, it was shortly after this, I believe it was around the end of summer when tragedy struck our family. My sister, CAROLYN'S bleeding got out of control. We did not have a car back then, so my dad hitched his tractor to a box trailer, and the whole family packed up, and drove about two and half miles to the farm of the local bush pilot, who had a small airplane. My sister was a brave little girl and did not make a fuss about anything. She was put in the cockpit with Mr. BATES, the pilot. I do not recall any family member accompanying her on her flight to Saskatoon, which had the best hospital in the province for treating cancer at the time. My parents took my older brother, and me to live with my dad's parents. We stayed at our grandparents' house for about two or three months and were cared for by our uncles and aunts, while my parents went by bus to Saskatoon.

It was a cold evening day in November 1953, when I saw my sister again. It was the most traumatic event for my young mind to absorb. My brother and I were ushered into one of the cold rooms of our grandparent's house where several family members were assembled. They were crying loudly, and I did not know why. My parents were there, and they also were crying. I could see that there was a little white coffin in the room, and in it was my sister. She was not moving. I touched her face, and her hands that were put together on top of her body. She felt cold. I called out to her, but she did not respond, and I did not know why. Eventually I was told that she had died, and she was not coming home again. She had gone to heaven, (her spirit that is). I cried uncontrollably, and I had this hopeless, sad feeling. The funeral was a very sad, sad event, and it stuck in my memory and prepared me for the numerous funerals I would attend in the future.

At about this time my brother, Rodney turned one year old. After the funeral we returned to our little house on the prairie where there was a big void in the family. I believe that my mother suffered the most with the tragic loss of a daughter. Life just carried on.

Chapter 3

COUNTRY SCHOOL/CHILDHOOD NEAR DISASTERS

My older brother, Chris, and I went to a little one room country school supposedly named after a Ukrainian family, called LYSENKO, which had about twenty students ranging from grade 1 to Grade 8. My father was the local school trustee, and for that year my brother, and I were to perform clean up duties at the school, which consisted of sweeping the floors every night, cleaning up the chalkboards, and dusting the school desks early in the morning before our classmates came to school. During the cold winter months after some instruction from our father, my brother, and I would have to start the coal furnace, and heat up the classroom. We were in luck most of the time as there were burning embers left over from the previous day. Of course, there were the weekend duties, which were to muck out the barn where some students kept their horses which were hitched up to a sled that brought them to school. Our winter school recesses were used to dig snow tunnels which provided some amusement. We also played a game of winter soccer. I never knew the rules of soccer, and I believe no one else knew the rules that well either, other than to choose two sides, and kick the ball between the goal posts. I received the first four years of my schooling in this little prairie school called LYSENKO SCHOOL.

The community expanded, and the decision was made to shut down Lysenko School, and transport us farm kids to Theodore School, approximately five miles away. It was an eye opener for us farm kids, but we fitted in pretty quickly by beating the crap out of most of the "think you're tough" town kids. We made new friends. I was an average student. I found it a bit of a challenge trying to get my homework done during the late evenings with the kerosene lamp for my source of light. I could only get my homework done after my farm chores were done which were performed every day in the morning, and evening and which consisted of herding the cows into the barn, and then milking them, and feeding the pigs and chickens. There was additional farm work especially throughout the spring, summer, and fall seasons which consisted of planting, and weeding which seemed like acres of vegetable gardens, and helping my dad with cutting, and gathering of the hay for the winter food source for the cattle, and other farm animals. Harvest time was more of a challenge for us farm kids as there were long hours helping with shovelling grain and helping out with break downs of the combines/threshing machines.

I must point out that I lived in a unique period of time on the Prairies. In my earlier years I recall my father farming using horses to pull the plough, and the cultivator to turn the soil. Then there was a brief time where I recall my dad driving one of those heavy metal pioneer tractors with steel wheels. It just plowed through the small trees and stumps. It seemed like the next year after that he got a small Massey Harris Model 22 rubber-tired tractor with some new farm implements. When it came time for harvesting, we used a harvesting machine called a binder which cut the wheat and oat fields and assembled the stalks of wheat and oats into bundles called sheaves. These sheaves would be dropped in stacks of six bundles. Then came the stooking, a term referred to someone coming along after, and arranging the bundles (heads of the grain) to stand upright to dry up in the sun. I remember doing this when I must have been around ten years old. I recall this being no fun at all, as you would quite often encounter the odd garter snake or mice in, or near the bundles. They were harmless, but I could not get used to their presence to this very day. Of course, the snakes were after their food source of little mice which were living in their glory with the grain as their food source. It was God's little creature's food chain.

The hot summer school holidays were filled with a tedious job of picking up rocks from the summer fallow (dirt / tilled) fields and dumping them in a pile along the fence line. We baked in the hot sun, and got numerous sun burns, which was mixed in with the blowing dirt. I had many a sad day, while I was in the fields picking up rocks, as some of my luckier friends were in the back of a farm truck driving past our farm waving to me, on their way to Good Spirit Lake for swimming lessons. Rock picking was a necessity as these rocks caused damage to binders, and later combines during the harvest time. Some rocks were pretty heavy for a youngster, but it built up the much, needed muscles when the time came to even the score with some school yard bullies. I do not ever recall losing a fight, and most often I would come to the aid of the underdog in the school yard brawls.

Moving on, my junior high school days offered a new interest in the game of baseball, which I thoroughly enjoyed. I played most of the field positions, and the one that I was not too good at, was being a pitcher. I believe I focused too much on the batter, who got to be on the receiving end of my fast ball pitch, and I ended up walking most of the opposing players. However, I had good hand/ ball coordination, and was usually put in the grand slam / cleanup slot which worked most of the time. I bated that ball pretty much out of the park. I remember coming home from a baseball game from a neighbouring town in the late evening, being dropped off at our school yard in town, and then having to cycle back five miles on a gravel road to our little house on the prairie. This was on a one speed heavy steel bike that took a lot of energy to get it moving fast on the loose gravel roads. I was feeling energetic most of the time having had a good time with friends, and if we won the game, it was even better. When I got home, my older brother let me know, he did not do my share of the farm chores, so I had to hurry, and get them done, sometimes in the dark. Once they were done, then came the school homework which I had to do in not a very good source of light. The source of light came from a small kerosene lamp, and the light was pretty dull.

I recall a time when our parents went to visit our neighbours, and left Chris and me at home. A short time after their departure, our Aunt Anne and Uncle Joe BARON came to visit us. It was a sunny summer day, so our Uncle Joe decided to hit us a few high fly balls in the air, and we would catch them. Well, he hit one in the direction of where my father had a hay cutting mower parked near his machine shop located in the farmyard. My father left the mower's 6-foot blade sticking out in about a twenty-five-degree angle. It had jagged knifelike metal pieces all along the blade with a larger jagged piece at the end of this six-foot blade. I ran to catch this ball with my eyes on the ball and was not watching as to where I was running. You guessed it-- I ran right into this knifelike jagged end piece, and my left thigh got stuck right into this blade. I was quite surprised and could feel a bit of the pain as my left thigh was stuck right into this metal end piece, and I could not pull it off without a real struggle. After a few attempts, I got free. My Uncle Joe and Chris ran to me in a panic as the blood started to pump out of my thigh. I cried a bit, but I did not panic. I guess I was disappointed that I missed the catch. However, I was more concerned that I'd just torn a hole into my new pair of jeans, and I was going to get spanked by my parents for wrecking them. We were poor then, and to tear up a new pair of jeans was a great burden on the family's finances. I believe God was at my side that day and limited my injuries. God built my character whereby I was able to handle future tragic incidents.

Another memorable moment in my young life was almost losing my eye while playing around with my friend Gary WALKER, and my brother Chris in and around our cow barn. We were playing a game of hide and seek. Well, it was my turn to find them. I found Gary hiding somewhere at the time with no problem. I went looking for Chris, and Gary was watching me. I opened the barn door and to my surprise, Chris stuck a three-tine pitchfork in my face. One of the tines struck me just above my right eyeball and pierced the skin in the eye lid. This was a dirty pitchfork to boot as you would expect. It was used in the barnyard chores, etc. A little blood came out, but God was at my side that day, and there were no permanent injuries. Chris was very surprised and felt rather dumbfounded as to why he taken the pitchfork in his hand and stabbed it at me. Gary witnessed this whole incident, and he reminded me of it at my mother's funeral in October 2014. Losing an eye would undoubtedly alter my journey in life and a career choice of joining the RCMP would have not happened. God looked after me again.

My older brother, Chris was having trouble with his studies in school, so he dropped out of school in grade 7, and got a job with a construction crew putting in the sewer pipeline in our town of Theodore. Finally, Theodore was moving into modernization with plumbing facilities. He then moved on to a high line hydroelectric construction crew, which eventually took him to Fort MacLeod, Alberta. He came home briefly during the winter months.

Chapter 4

MY CRAZY UNCLE ANDREW

We had a bit of an unpleasant incident with our father's younger brother, Andrew. Both my brother, Chris, and I worked his farm during our school summer holidays. He paid us a dollar an hour. My dad and Andrew had some monetary issues as well as Andrew did not like that my father was able to buy some pastureland from our drunken grandfather for a certain price, only to pay for it in instalments. Andrew also did not like that my father, being the oldest of the siblings, was able to get some of the farm tools, which he himself wanted.

On one particular day in one cold (1963) winter months, Chris and I went to retrieve some tools from our grandfather's farm that our father said were ours. We drove to our grandfather's farmhouse, and after meeting with our grandfather we told him that we come to pick up these tools. He took us to his workshop, and showed us where these tools were, and said that they belonged to our father. We loaded them into the trunk of Chris's car and started to drive home.

We got about a few hundred yards from the farm gate and were stopped on the road by our Uncle Andrew, who was driving his car in the opposite direction. He asked us what we were doing, so we told him. He said he wanted to see what we took. My brother opened up the trunk of his car, and Andrew grabbed this particular tool (tap and die set - used for threading bolts), and took it, and put it in the trunk of his car.

I told Andrew that my father had said these tools were ours, and even our grandfather said that they were ours. Chris, being a tall, fit guy was a bit scared to confront our somewhat crazy irate uncle. I was tough, and not scared to take on anybody, so I grabbed the tools from Andrew's car trunk just before he was about to slam it shut. I said they were ours and put them back in Chris's car trunk and slammed it shut.

I had turned around to get into Chris's car when I was confronted by Andrew who was in a fit of rage. I could see the anger in his face as he held an axe high over his head. With both his hands and in a swinging motion I could see the axe coming down to split me in half. I put up a block with my arms and grabbed the axe away from him and threw it into the nearby snowdrift. Andrew kept on screaming in his rage. Chris tried to talk to him and settle him down. I told Andrew I did not want to see him again, and that he'd better not come to our farm, or I would finish him off. It worked because I never saw him again until he died about three years later. This time I saw him in his coffin and made sure they threw him into the ground.

Chapter 5

MY RUNAWAY FROM HOME

Chris went on to a job in Fort Macleod, Alberta, and later wrote me a letter, saying that if I wanted to get a job working at the Trailer (mobile home) Factory he could get me on his crew. I do not recall if I told my parents what I intended on doing for the summer holidays, but it was the same every year - boring farm work with no pay. So, I got hold of my good friend, Gary Walker, who earlier had got fed up with school studies, and decided to drop out of school in grade 8. Gary who is nine days older than me and lived with his parents one mile away from our home, was my childhood friend. We have kept in touch with one another infrequently throughout our adult lives. Gary got a job as a night watchman on the dam project a few miles from our home. A few years later, Gary took an autobody repair course and ran a very successful autobody shop in Theodore.

Gary's parents brought a 1955 Ford car, and he drove it as his parents did not have a driver's license. So, the day before I was to write my final Grade 11 exam, I packed what little amount of clothes I had into a cardboard box, tied it up with binder twine (used for binding grain sheave bundles) and took it, and what little money I saved up, to school with me. Gary picked me up after school, and drove me to Yorkton, where I caught a Greyhound bus for Fort MacLeod Alta. Gary later informed my parents of my departure. They were quite disappointed with my leaving home.

I met my brother, Chris in Fort MacLeod. He drove me around the town, proudly driving his 1955 Pontiac. My brother stayed in a house where he got room and board, and I was welcomed to stay at the same accommodations, which were run by a very young couple. This couple had a male friend who lived in Calgary. He and his girlfriend came to visit them pretty much every weekend. He drove a 1958 Ford Thunderbird, and it was a most impressive car. One nice sunny Saturday I recall him taking me for a fast ride to Lethbridge, which was a short distance from Fort MacLeod. He showed me his skillful driving as we cruised along the highway at about 140 mph. It was my first interest to land speed that fast, and my interest in speed began.

Upon my arrival at Fort MacLeod, Chris took me to the Trailer Home Factory and was able to use his influence as a foreman of the ceiling department to get me working on his crew. I was making $1.35/hour. After I'd done this routine work with speed and precision for six weeks, the general foreman offered me a raise to $1.45/hour, and I was promoted to foreman of the ceiling department. Chris was moved to another department. About a week later, I told the general foreman that I thought I should return home to complete my high school education. He said he was sorry to lose me as an employee but agreed with me about finishing my schooling. He told me that I had a job with the company should I wish to return the following year.

My two months in Fort Macleod were a good learning curve. There, I met new friends, some who were natives from the Blood Indian Reserve, Joe and his brother, Roy SCOUT. Joe ran a local gas station. He drove a 1958 Ford, retractable convertible. It was a beautiful car. On numerous occasions I hung around with him, eventually meeting his younger brother, Roy, who was my age. There were a few times that they managed to get me onto their reserve undetected. The law at that time was that no white man was to be on the reserve after sunset. We usually had several dozen cases of beer and partied with the local girls.

On one occasion I got to see a Pow Wow / Dance ceremony, which at the time was pretty impressive. Being young warriors at the time while the Vietnam war was going on in mid 1960's, we both made a verbal agreement going Stateside joining the US Army or Marines together and fight the Communists, which was big news of the time. Roy's cousin was already in the U.S. military and that sparked our interest in joining up. Roy and I corresponded through mail a few times when I went back home, after terminating my job at the Fort Macleod Trailer Factory.

When I finished high school, I returned to Fort Macleod, and got hold of Roy. He changed his mind, and was not interested in joining the army, as he had gotten accepted into a college in Calgary. I had got accepted into the Royal Canadian Air Force, which was one of my dream careers, but did not pursue this opportunity, as the pay was not very good. I wanted to fly fighter jets, but I was a bit too tall for the crowded cockpit.

Vietnam would have been a whole adventurous experience for both of us, and it also could have come with some very devastating consequences. I lost contact with Roy as my life was moving in a different direction than his. Years later, while I was at the RCM Police Academy in Ottawa, I ran into Joe and Roy's younger sister who was at the Academy for a course in preparation for her for a job as the native police chief of the Blood Indian Nation. She said that Roy became an alcoholic, and his life had gone nowhere. It was a tragedy to hear such news when I thought he had a potential to achieve something of great quality.

My last year of high school was uneventful. I studied as best as I could, but my marks were average, and entrance into the medical profession was completely out of the question. Farming was not for me, so I decided to go to live with my brother, Chris and his wife, Bea in small dirty coal mining town, that was known at the time as Michel, B.C., and which was eventually incorporated into today's town of Sparwood, B.C.

Chapter 6

MY FIRST LONG TERM JOB

I was down to my last twenty dollars when I applied for a job as a junior accountant with the CROWSNEST INDUSTRIES MINING COMPANY. I got accepted, and my job was to be the accounts payable clerk for their purchasing department. I later learned that I had tested better in the math questions than an experienced person who had some accounting experience. I managed to hitch a ride to work with a sexy, vivacious, young married Canadian/Italian woman, who lived in my neighbourhood.

Her boss was formerly from Regina, Sask., and the one who had hired me. She drove a new Studebaker sedan which came from her husband's dealership. She was a bit of a wild driver, especially during wintertime. She would drive into a snowbank, and I would have to end up pushing the car out of the snowbank. She was great fun, and we had a lot of laughs together.

I met her younger brother, and we became good friends. Unfortunately, he was sadly killed in a car accident about a year later. It happened on the day before Good Friday and the Easter holiday. He was sent on an errand by the Catholic priest to pick up the holy water from the Fernie Catholic Church. He asked me if I would like to go with him for the ride, but I had other things to do, and did not go. So, he asked another friend to accompany him. He was driving the Catholic priest's car on this journey. Unfortunately, on the way back from Fernie on the straight stretch of highway, he and his friend ended up in a head on crash where they both died, as well as a family of five that ran into them. It was a horrible scene, and a shock to the Fernie, and Starwood community, particular the Catholic parish. I think God was looking out for me again, and I avoided another brush with death.

The community healed and moved on. A short time later, another friend asked me to join him, and two other friends for a ride to a neighbouring town of Blairmore, Alberta, in his red 1963 Chevy, two door hardtop. En route on Highway No. 3 to Blairmore they may have been going too fast around the twisting narrow highway, lost control, and drove through the not so sturdy barricade into the icy, cold CROWSNEST LAKE. The RCMP found the three of them dead in the car, which was just hanging on a ledge. They had drowned. Had they gone beyond the ledge, they would have never been recovered, as it is a very deep lake. It was my luck that I refused to go with them that day. I think it was God's way to prepare me for what was in store for me in the days ahead.

I bought my first car, a 1957 Buick Special, four door hardtop for $350.00. To me it was a beautiful car - blue with white trim, and red patten leather interior. Gas was cheap, approximately $ .45/$ .50 per gallon. Yes, we were using gallons as a form of measure in those days. But this car had engine problems, and oil was expensive, so it used more oil than gas. It was always fill the oil, and check the gas. I was very impressed with this Buick, although it was heavy, and looked like an army tank, and if you pressed the gas pedal down, it went into passing gear, and you would go to about 120 mph in no time flat. It was a fantastic, beautiful ride. I wish I had that car today, and that I restored it to its original state.

I eventually traded in the Buick for a small Chevy Corvair with a rear engine similar to the Volkswagen cars of the time.

Life in Sparwood became boring, so I decided to move to Fernie, B.C. I got a room, and board place in Mrs. Marie WAUGH's house. She was a very hardworking woman in her fifties doing maid/cleaning services for several households. Mrs. WAUGH had two useless children, and a lazy, drunken husband, Bill, who occasionally worked as a barman at one of the local hotels. Sometimes I would not get enough food, or a decent meal. Mrs WAUGH did the best she could on a small budget, and we all got by. I admired her hard work, and caring spirit, and I basically felt she got a bad rap in life. She was a great soul. Her husband was basically useless.

I had met a young engineer, Lok SHARMA, about my age while working at CROWSNEST INDUSTRIES. He and his brother, Pal SHARMA, both engineers immigrated from India. We had great fun together, and I think I corrupted his Indian cultural upbringing. I had a car, and every weekend, we would travel to either Cranbrook, or into the nearest towns in the USA, which was a short distance from Fernie, as well as Lethbridge and Calgary. We would consume a lot of beer on our trips as well as meet a lot of young women, which did not work in our favour. I suppose it was a cultural shock, and prejudice on the white women's part, but he was my friend, and I would not let him down. I should have taken up his offer to travel with him around India and meet his family and friends. I eventually did travel to India years later with my second wife, Caroline who is of Armenian heritage born in Calcutta. Lok would eventually move to Edmonton to pursue his master's degree in engineering at the University of Alberta.

To subsidize my low salary, and desire for more money, I took on a part time job working in a small insurance company, called LOWE'S INSURANCE, run by a woman, named Alta LOWE. She really liked me, and before long, sold me a life insurance policy, which I cashed in a few years later, because I needed the money. I became great friends with her only child, Caroline, who was a registered nurse in Edmonton, and travelled often to Fernie, B.C., to visit her parents on several occasions. It was a brother/sister relationship. She had a great sense of humour and was always laughing. Her father bought her a car, and she wanted to drive it back to Edmonton during a very cold winter. She wanted me to accompany her on her journey to Edmonton as the highway through the Crowsnest Pass was very treacherous with blowing snow, and ice on the highway surface.

I thought I would take this trip, and get to visit my friend, Lok, despite the fact I was suffering from a severe flu. Caroline being a nurse said she would look after me, and once we got to Edmonton, she would get me the best medication that the nursing staff get as they deal with a lot of severe illnesses, most of which came from the Northwest Territories. I was driving the car, and sure enough we encountered severe driving conditions with blowing snow, and icy roads. We got through the canyon into Alberta, and then the weather got even more severe, with cold high velocity blowing wind that seemed to come right into the car. We were freezing, with blankets wrapped around us. I was shivering so much that Caroline cuddled up next to me to supply me with body heat, and we carried on. We had enough gas to make it to Edmonton, and it seemed like we were the only vehicle on the road at times.

We arrived in Edmonton, and Caroline got the medicine from the nurse's residence, and had me checked into a hotel. I was in bad shape. She told me to take the medicine, and it would prob-ably knock me out for a while, but I would be OK the next day. She was right. The hotel room was stone cold with very little heat coming through the heat registers. The next day was a bit sunny with freezing cold weather.

I called Lok, and he came to my hotel. I had great laugh when I first saw Lok walking towards the hotel. Here was Lok, from a sunny, warm India, enduring his first ever severe cold weather in Canada's northern region. Lok, who was about 5'5 in height was wrapped up in a huge bulky parka. I could see his brown face with icicles on his hood. He was a sight, and we both had a good laugh. He wanted to show me where he was attending classes, so we went over to the university, and had a lunch, and a nice visit. I saw him one other time after this when I visited him in Fernie, one year after I joined the RCMP. He got married to a young woman from India and was now working for KAISER RESOURCES. Our lives moved on in different directions.

The Elk Valley, where CROWSNEST INDUSTRIES had their logging operation was not immune to forest fires. So, one summer season, they were looking for any available personnel to help with the firefighting. I had some holiday time booked up, so I spent my two vacation weeks fighting forest fires. I was teamed up with some older men, who were around my father's age. New immigrants from Italy, they had some difficulty with speaking the English language. I was put in charge of this small group to fill out their time sheets, and to do my best in explaining what we were required to do as a team in putting out these spot fires. We had a lot of fun in amongst this hard work. I enjoyed the interaction with the new immigrants.

While working at CROWSNEST INDUSTRIES, one of my accounting bosses, Norm Crossfield, suggested that I join the local Kinsmen Social Club. I did and enjoyed going to the bars after the meetings with the older Kinsmen members. I was nineteen at the time, and the legal drinking age was twenty-one.

As the Kinsmen Club sponsored the local baseball team, and had no coach, I took on the challenge. I took on a bunch of young boys, some with delinquent problems, some from single mother/ broken homes, some from recent immigrant families. I turned those boys into a successful baseball team that would win the trophy they had strived for the previous five years. I had a lot of fun with this group of young boys, and I think they appreciated me for leading them to their success in winning the league cup. On a number of occasions they would pile into my then newer car (I traded in the Buick) a 1964 two-door Chevy Corvair, and

I would drive them slowly a short distance away to the local ice-cream parlour, and spend what little money I had, buying them ice-cream. Back in those days we could get away with driving a lot of passengers in a car. I sometimes had seven of them in my little car. The rest of the team ran along on the sidewalk to the ice-cream stand for their treats.

The local RCMP members would make their usual hotel bar checks, and I managed not to get thrown out for being underage. A short time later two local RCMP members joined the Kinsmen Club, and again after the meeting we would go to the bars. Well, being an honest guy, I figured I better inform them that I was underage. Cst. Jerry SIMMONDS said he'd seen me in bars before, and thought I looked of age, so he was prepared to overlook this bit of indiscretion.

So, I went to the local bar with the gang, and then Cst. SIMMONDS, who sat next to me, made me an offer I could not refuse. He suggested that I join the RCMP and come and see him at the RCMP Detachment the next day. I was to fill out an application. He said the process for acceptance would take about a year before I would know if I met the RCMP standards. He said that three out of 100 candidates would be selected, and one would get accepted.

Before long, the coal mining division of CROWSNEST INDUSTRIES was acquired by KAISER RESOURCES, from Oakland, Calif., and I moved with some of the staff in the transition. I became a cost accountant for the maintenance and operations department. I worked for two very qualified men, who I greatly respected. They in turn appreciated my accounting abilities.

However, accounting became a bit boring, and I had one superior, named Peter, (bald headed asshole) from the accounting department, who mostly walked around the office, with a bunch of papers in his hand, and did a lot of talking, and very little work. He came from Castlegar, B.C. He would take some of my accounting ideas, and take them to our accounting boss, and say he'd came up with them. This was before computers were invented, and accounting figures were done on handwritten ledgers. Other senior accountants recognized what was going on with this asshole, and they knew that those were my ideas. Eventually this uppity attitude of this asshole, made me realize how some office politics play out, and I had had about enough of this sort of work, having become a bit restless.

I expressed an interest in personnel work. I had met Gene Klemmer, a tall, larger than life Texan, who was the KAISER INDUSTRIES general manager of personnel from their Oakland office. He was responsible for setting up the KAISER RESOURCES' office staff at the Elk Valley operations. In our meetings, he asked me about my accounting skills and hobbies, etc. Gene knew I coached minor baseball, a USA favourite pass time, so he invited me to his home, and wanted me to meet his son. I got to know him in a more personal way. Gene told me that his wife was an alcoholic. They were a much older couple with a young son. Gene wanted me to look after his son and teach him the game of base-ball. He travelled a lot throughout the world for KAISER and was unable to spend the much, needed time with his family. His son was a nice young fella, a bit shy, but determined to play baseball. I would pick him up for the baseball practices and introduce him to the tough young (some delinquent) boys on my team. Some ridiculed him that he did not know how to play baseball, after all he was an American. I stepped in to settle the harassment. Before long they accepted him. It meant a lot to me, and I also knew it meant a lot to Gene. It was a challenge, and a hurdle that we as a team accomplished. I often wondered in later years if these young guys in their adult life had any thoughts about their early years, where they were in their present time, and the fun they had as young boys.

Chapter 7

ABDUCTED BY A PLAYBOY MODEL

In 1969, I was not well informed with the Criminal Code of Canada, but I knew the basic laws surrounding robbery, murder, thefts, frauds, assaults, and some motor vehicle infractions. But abduction/kidnapping was not really on my mind until it happened to me, and this was a rather innocent, humorous experience in my short life at the time.

While I was employed at KAISER RESOURCES, one of my coworkers wanted me to meet his wife's girlfriend. He described her as being very good looking, a year or two older than me, and said she'd posed as a Playboy centrefold model. He told me that she would be a good fun date for me, but I was NOT to mention anything about knowing she'd worked as a Playboy centrefold model etc. So, he arranged a meeting one night at a local hotel pub, and there I met him, his wife and her girlfriend. I must say the girlfriend was stunning and beautiful. I had not been around much or travelled around much in my life at the time. We had a few drinks, etc. It seemed that we all drank a fair amount of beer, but we knew roughly when to stop, so that we were able to navigate driving our vehicles when it came time to drive home. As the evening ended, I said I'd better walk home, as I had to get up for work in the morning. I did not have a car at the time.

This girlfriend had driven up to this hotel/pub in her 1965 Mustang convertible. So, she said that she would drive me home. I accepted the offer and told her where I lived at a room-and-board house not far from the hotel. I directed her on the route to my home, which was one block off the No. 3 main highway that ran through Fernie from points westward beyond Cranbrook BC., and eastward through to the Alberta border.

She seemed familiar and had a good sense of direction as to where she was going. As it was the same highway, she had travelled on to visit her friends with whom we had just spent an evening. She drove right past my home, and headed straight for the highway, without stopping for stop signs. She turned her car in the direction towards Cranbrook, and other USA destinations. We were laughing, as we had just consumed a quantity of beer. I told her to turn around as she drove past my place. She was laughing, and said she was taking me to her home in the States. I said that I could not go, as I had to go to work in the morning, and if my landlady did not find me home, she might get worried, and call the RCMP. Also, that I was recruited by the RCMP, and was scheduled for training in February. She kept on laughing and driving on, full speed ahead. I did not panic as she was laughing, and kept saying she wanted me, and that was that I should not worry about the money, etc. I felt that at some point she would turn around, but that was not the case.

In a short time, we drove across the Canada/USA border. I do not recall what transpired there, as border crossings between Canada and the USA were a lot different than they are now. I eventually convinced her that if I did not show up for work and my landlady called the RCMP, they would start looking for me, and eventually they may call the FBI, as she was an American who was last seen with me. This could result in an international incident. It was late into the night, so she decided to turn around. We drove across the border and headed for Cranbrook, BC. We were tired so we spent a night at a motel.

She eventually drove me to my home in the late afternoon. Sure enough, my landlady had called the RCMP, and they had started looking for me. I called the RCMP and told them the story. We all had a good laugh. She carried on to her friend's place and stayed there for a few days. We had another date, as she hoped I would change my mind, and go with her to the States. I said I had a career opportunity and did not want to miss it. This was the same time that United States was involved in the Vietnam War, and a lot of young men were drafted, and had gone over there. That was the end of this fun abduction.

Chapter 8

CARRYING ON

I decided that I needed to get into some top physical condition before joining up with RCMP, so I made a decision to give up my job at KAISER. No sooner had I given my notice then I had a call from a local chartered accountant in Fernie, B.C. He offered me a job at his office. I went to see him, and he made me an offer of working at his firm, and then taking a chartered accountant's course by correspondence. His firm would then send me to university for the final year, expenses paid, and then I would get my CA degree. I asked him to give me his biggest business account, I would do all the required work, put the business ledger, etc., in order, and he could go over it to finalize everything. I put everything in order in about two weeks; however, I did not find this too inspiring, so I told him I was going to quit.

I then joined a road paving construction company and took on a labour job. The owner found out I had an accounting background and took me off the heavy labour to do some nice respectable work, in his view. I was to go to all the new households in this new sub-division and measure out the driveway's and convince these households that they needed paved driveways. I was a hit. I sold out the whole subdivision. I met a lot of the bored housewives who had other plans, making it clear to me that their executive husbands were busy travelling for KAISER RESOURCES, and they were available. I gave them no indication that I would jeopardize my job. Business was business, I was selling paved driveways, and they bought them. I got their driveways paved!!!!!! Everybody was happy and I disappeared a few months later.

I later joined a construction crew building apartment buildings. It was heavy labour of pick and shovel work, so I put my heart and soul into it. Before long the superintendent of the apartment project found out that I knew how to drive a tractor, as he needed an operator to run a tractor backhoe. I managed to get this old tractor/backhoe working and dug the trench for the drainage around the perimeter of the apartment buildings. The superintendent was a very nice guy. He recognized my operating skills, and he suggested a better job that paid higher wages than what his company was paying me. He put me in touch with another construction company that had better up to date equipment, and they needed operators. I was hired immediately and was given a service pickup to drive to and from work. They paid me much more money than my previous job. This construction company also recognized that I had some accounting skills and requested if I would assist them in their bookkeeping, which I obliged. They even made me an offer of partnership with their company. I informed them that I had made some previous plans to go to Hawaii for a two-week holiday, but said I would think it over.

I had a great time on Waikiki beach and got a great suntan. I returned to Fernie and told the construction company that I had previously gotten accepted into the RCMP and was scheduled to report at the Regina Depot Division on February 4, 1970. Those cold, freezing days fixing broken equipment on the backhoe with sometimes bare hands made me decide to join the RCMP for a lot less money, and give up a possible partnership in a growing construction company. I made some serious big money in this construction company, and it was hard to turn them down.

Chapter 9

MY CAREER IN THE RCMP

On February 4, 1970, I boarded a flight for Regina, Sask. I arrived in the late evening at the RCMP Depot Division. It was very cold. The Saskatchewan wind was howling, and there were snow drifts everywhere. For a brief moment, I wondered if I had made the right decision. I reported to the guard house and met with the very stern NCO in charge who assigned me to my barracks. I was in Troop 15, regimental number 27726 (this number stays with you for the rest of your life). There began a chapter in my life that I reflect upon as being the most eventful, rewarding time in my life.

I joined thirty-one other eager ready young men from various parts of Canada in a thirty-two man barracks in "B" block. Every evening at 21:45 hours we were to stand at attention in our underwear next to our neatly made bed while the duty sergeant walked up, and down both sides (fifteen army cots on each side of the dorm) checking the occasional closet making sure our uniforms were in order, our shoes were spit-shined, etc. When he came to me, he stopped, and asked me where I got my suntan. I told him I spent two weeks in Hawaii about a month previous. This very stern sergeant looked at me with his steely eyes and said, "Do you know how long I have to work to afford a holiday like that?" I said, "No sir." He asked me where I got my money to afford this holiday and I told him that I worked for a construction company, and for about 2 weeks of work it pretty much paid for my holiday. He gave me an aggravated look, and I knew he was not amused. He then moved on. I often thought about what was going through his mind, and the resentment he perhaps held for me, with him working in the RCMP for such low wages, and here was this young recruit sporting a suntan having spent a two-week holiday in Hawaii. I made it a point to avoid him during my time in Depot Division, as the senior personnel could often revoke your pass for slight indiscretion, and you would not be able to leave the base for a bit of partying at the bars on the weekend.

This six-month training course was an eye opener, and at the end of it, most of us agreed that every young man should go through this sort of training. We all made a whole lot of friends, and we learned to work together as a team, and supported one another. This was during the hippy, pot smoking era. During this time most young people had chosen different paths in life, and sometimes with no direction whatsoever; however, looking across the human spectrum today some individuals at that time were quite messed up. It was the Liberal way of thinking, more freedom, less punishment for crime. The Liberal way of thinking seems to be that chaos on the streets makes way for more jobs in the medical, educational or judicial fields. This was explained to me at my Major Crime course which I attended several years later at the RCMP Academy in Ottawa. The instructor of that particular class was a lawyer, who was at time the president (person in charge) of the Ontario Bar Association. He said he could not say this to his peers, but he felt safe to say this in a room full of cops, who immediately objected to what he said. After a minute or so, we all had a different perspective. There were jobs for us.

One profound moment within the two weeks of our training, we had two members of our troop quit. One of our instructors, Cpl. WENDEL in full RCMP uniform walked into the front of our classroom, turned around, and faced the class in his very stern, disciplined, erect stature. He was bald headed and had this very NAZI look (as you see in the wartime movies). He addressed the class by saying that "You have had two members from your troop quit. The Canadian Government spent a lot of money to get you here for training. If anyone else feels that they cannot take a bullet, then they could leave, there is the door (he pointed to the back of the classroom), you have five minutes". He then sat down at his desk in front of the classroom, took off his wristwatch, and looked down on his lesson paperwork. I was sitting in the back to one side of the classroom and had a good view of the other classmates as they looked at each other to see, who were the coward's heading for the door. Some smiled at each other, some had concerned looks on their faces. Of the remaining thirty members, two of us got into gunfights during our service. One of the members was Jeff TOURAND, and the other one was me. You can read about my story later on in chapter 27.

Unfortunately, Jeff brought on his injury in his gunfight by not securing his prisoner properly. He arrested a man for a violation, handcuffed him, and placed him in the front seat of his police cruiser, and then drove to the detachment. In route to the detachment, the prisoner reached over, and grabbed Jeff's service revolver. A struggle ensued between Jeff, and the prisoner while Jeff attempted to stop the car. The prisoner managed to get one shot off which struck Jeff in the abdomen area. Jeff survived the ordeal, but later became addicted to medication for his injuries. He unfortunately had a short career, and later died at a young age.

My first posting was Gibson's, B.C. As I did not own a car, I hooked a ride with one of my best friends of Troop 15, Cst. Hank KWIATKOWSKI. He had this amazing, threshold to accept physical pain, which in normal circumstances most people could not bear. He also had the amazing capacity for consuming a large quantity of liquor and being able to walk a pretty straight line. A lot of people during the early 70's had quite different views of liquor consumption and driving. We tried to be discreet, and careful at the same time, knowing that the RCMP would not condone bad conduct. We would be subsequently charged, loose our jobs and not be able to get a respectable job again.

Hank, a short time later in his RCMP career, had a moment of poor judgment, and got involved in a small theft, and was dismissed from the force. I briefly kept in touch with him, and then I saw his life had spiraled out of control. He got separated from his wife, and two children, and later divorced. He got involved with narcotics, and his life came to end a short time later. Perhaps a lot Hank's problems occurred in his childhood, having lost both parents at very young age. I believe he was a teenager at the time when that happened, and he was in charge of looking after his younger siblings, who were probably also brought up by other relatives. Hank related his family situation to me while we were training at the RCMP Depot Division. He said he tried to keep his family together, but it was not easy. Prior to being accepted in the RCMP, Hank was a salesman selling combines, and other farm machinery in Manitoba. He had the gift of the gab so to speak and was quite a talker. He must have been quite a salesman.

My first impressions of Gibson's, and the surrounding area in the middle of a beautiful month of August was just unbelievable. For a prairie guy it was an awesome paradise. My living accommodations were in a two-man bedroom barracks, with a small bathroom next to the jail cell, where we had many visitors. At most times these prisoners were very rowdy, and created a lot of noise, especially during my sleep hours. So, it was up to the constable who was inconvenienced to settle the prisoner down. The "norm" was to enter the cell area, and physically make him to do "the chicken". After the prisoner was tossed around the inside walls and sometimes hitting the metal cell cage, they eventually got the message, and quietened down. I recall one such prisoner, whom when I released him the following morning, he apologized for his behaviour, saying he drank too much liquor, and that when he does consume too much liquor, he goes out of control. He shook my hand on the way out of the detachment holding cells and promised to behave himself in the future. I never had any problem with him for the rest of my time in Gibson's.

Chapter 10

MY FIRST EXPOSURE TO A PERSON GETTING SHOT

One memorable event which I experienced in Gibson's was getting a frantic call from a woman late one evening, claiming that her husband threatened to kill her, and anyone else that crossed him. He apparently took off in his car and was determined to carry out his act. I was a young constable and was working alone at the time. All the other detachment members were attending a farewell party for one of the departing Sechelt Detachment members, and there was no way to get a hold of any of them. Our radio reception was very minimal at best to none. I did manage to get a call through for assistance from two Sechelt members coming back to their Detachment from Pender Harbour. In the meantime, I was making my way to this woman's house when I spotted the suspect's car coming towards me at a high rate of speed. I turned around and chased him at speeds of about 80 mph on the narrow roads, and over little hills around Gibson's. It was exciting, and a real adrenal rush. I later compared this driving episode to that of the famous Hollywood actor of that time, Steve McQUEEN. In the movie called "Bulitt" he was driving in a similar manner along the streets of San Francisco.

The suspect eventually stopped on a dark road and jumped out of his car with a large butcher/hunting knife in each of his hands. He first stood by his car and told me to shoot him. I got out of my police car, with the car lights shining on him, and told him to drop his knives, and we could talk. I was quite taken back, because I had met this man several times for coffee at the BC Ferry Terminal. He was one of the supervisors there, and prior to this time, he seemed like a very nice guy. This was now a whole different scenario. He went berserk, and told me to shoot him, or he would kill me. I told him I would not do that. He then raised both of his hands holding the knives over his head, and started to shout, and ran towards me. He looked very determined to kill me. I quickly got back into the police car and locked the door. It was very tense at this moment, as here was a guy who I briefly met, and respected, and now I was faced with the possibility of shooting him if I did not get him to drop the knives. He then decided to get back into his car, and then drove like a maniac at speeds of 80/90 mph over the hills, and narrow streets of Gibson's.

It was a wild scary ride. I did not know how this was going to play out, but I carried on. I got on my police radio and attempted to call the Sechelt Detachment members to find out where they were. They were still quite a distance from Gibson's. All of a sudden on a dark road the suspect again came to a stop. He got out of his car with the knives in each hand and started shouting at me to shoot him. When he saw that I was not responding to his desire, he got back into his vehicle, and we continued on this wild ride. I radioed to the Sechelt members my position, and the direction the suspect will most likely take. By this time, they gained a lot of ground.

We were heading north on Pratt Rd., so they said they would situate their police vehicle across the road and block his path. Sure, enough the suspect, and I came flying over a small hill at a high rate of speed. The Sechelt members had their police car across the road with its red lights flashing.

The suspect came to complete stop and got out his car with both those big knives in each of his hands. He continued to shout for us to shoot him. Cst. Ron MANGAN leaned over the trunk of his police car, and levelled his revolver, and did exactly as the suspect had requested. He fired one shot into the suspect's thigh. The suspect dropped the knives and slumped down on his knees. I ran up and grabbed the knives while Cst. MANGAN, and Cst. Darryl KETTLES grabbed the suspect and took him to the Sechelt hospital. I drove the suspect's car to the side of the road and parked it there to be removed later the next day. I then went to see the suspect's wife to inform her of what happened to her husband.

The suspect's wife let me into her house. I told her that I had some sad news to tell her and related what happened. The only everlasting statement that I remember from her in this whole incident was, "you should have aimed higher". She continued to tell me of a previous incident, where her husband took a knife, and was going to slice open her stomach. She grabbed a pillow and placed it in front of her just in time as he made the slicing motion. Her husband sliced open the pillow. She managed to get away that time. She said that he is a nice person only when he takes his medication. On this particular day he did not take his medication and went "NUTS".

This fellow went into a psychiatric hospital for about a month. Shortly after his arrival at the hospital, and before being released from the institution, he wrote the Sechelt members, and me a letter of how grateful he was that we did not kill him. He apologized for his behaviour and said he would not do it again. We, at the detachment felt differently, and had discussions which centred around if a similar situation arose again, that somebody better aim higher, and put an end to this lady's misery.

I did meet with this individual on few occasions since this incident, and he was a very decent person. It was like this never happened. I got transferred to Powell River a short time later, and I heard that this individual had gone berserk again and was hospitalized. I do not know what happened to his wife, or of his state of mind since.

Chapter 11

KISSED BY AN ADMIRER/ GETTING SHOT AT

On occasions our Detachment commander had us do liquor offences enforcement checks at the Roberts Creek Dance Hall. A local hippy group, or a representative of them, who was a creditable person with no criminal record would get a liquor permit which was approved by the Detachment commander. The permit had to be for some sort of a charity, and certain percentage of the proceeds definitely had to be sent to that particular charity. We had to ensure that things were on the up, and up so to speak. There was usually a whole lot of marihuana smoking going on.

On one such occasion I attended at the dance hall. I walked in my full RCMP uniform, and got a lot of heckling, and was called a bunch of nasty names. Some individuals were trying to get me to check them, so they would just push me, or accidentally hit me. It was quite common in this sort of environment. They tried to make me scared, or nervous so that I would leave them alone. I walked around and met with the individual who took out the permit.

They were the only ones as well as some of their good friends, who were respectful towards me.

As I was walking out of the dance hall, there was this tall, attractive African American woman, who in the past dealings always wanted to kiss me, heading right for me. It was the hippy era, free love and all that. Well sure enough she caught me when I was a bit off guard, and put her arm around my neck, leaned in, and kissed my cheek. She had a big smile on her face, and no doubt was happy with her accomplishment. I was a good sport about it, and gently removed her arm, and said thanks, and that I had to go. She just kept on smiling, and everyone around who saw this cheered her on.

According to the government statistics, Gibson's in the early 1970's had the most unstable people per capita in B.C. So, there was a lot of excitement for a young policeman working in the area.

Another memorable event was when then Cst. Don BROST, and I got a complaint of someone shooting near the Peninsula Hotel late one evening. We drove out to the vicinity of the suspect's house and parked the police car with the headlights on. We got out and walked a bit of a distance towards the suspect's house. All of sudden the suspect opened the door of his house, and levelled a rifle in our direction, and started shooting at us. We ducked for cover, as the bullets were whistling through the trees near us, ran back to the police car, and drove back to the detachment. We advised the i/c of Gibson's Det., Cpl. Lou BIGGEMAN of what we had encountered. He decided that we wait until the next morning, and go down, and surprise the suspect.

Early in the morning we went to his house, and pushed open his door, and got him out of bed. He was well known to us. He sobered up somewhat and cooperated with us. We seized his several loaded rifles, and ammo which he had positioned next to entrance of his house. No charges were laid. The matter was solved quite differently. As he was the sole provider for his large family, and agreed to forfeit his guns to us, and not go crazy again, he was set free. We now had stories to tell our friends of our survival.

Unfortunately, years later, Don during his last years in RCMP discovered he had heart problems, and had to have a heart bypass; however, that was not the end of his health problems. After his retirement from the RCMP, he got a job in a company as Security management for a short time. One day he collapsed in his yard, and his wife thought it had something to do with his heart. Upon examination, it was found that he had brain cancer. He suffered through the chemo treatments, unfortunately the cancer won out in his ordeal, and he died in his mid sixties.

Not long after I arrived at the Gibson's Det., an outlaw motorcycle gang member murdered someone in Vancouver. We got some information that he got on a tugboat or a yacht and was headed for Gibson's. A number of Vancouver City Police members together with some Vancouver RCMP Plain clothes members came to Gibson's, and started making enquiries, and searching several boats to no avail. They stopped for the night, but I was to assume working all night by myself, searching various suspicious boats, and abandoned buildings along the waterfront etc. I walked the ramp of where some boats were docked and commenced checking the unlocked cabins.

The next morning when I returned to work with only a couple of hours of sleep, I was advised that the suspect took off in a boat and was later apprehended. The boat which he had stolen was one of boats I checked that night that had its cabin door locked, so I do not know if he was in the boat at the time when I was making the checks. I think GOD was on my side that particular time, and HE has been my protector on numerous occasions since then.

Chapter 12

MY FIRST EXPOSURE TO A FATAL PLANE CRASH

I had several blood and guts incidents in Gibson's. One such time was when I was having much needed lunch at the only available good diner in Gibson's. It was opened for lunch and dinner, and it usually shut down by 8 p.m., promptly (I starved quite a number of evenings). I started eating my lunch and was in the middle of my meal when I got a call that there had been an small airplane crash not far up the road from where I was having my lunch. I paid for my lunch and took off in a hurry to where I found the small aircraft in flames. It was a very horrible scene. It was very hot. I could see two human bodies on fire with their arms stretched out. I could not rescue them. Eventually the local fire department came out and put out the fire. The bodies were removed to the local morgue.

Later that same weekend there had been a motorcycle accident in the Pender Harbour area and both the male driver, and his younger female passenger ended up in this same morgue. I was advised that the male motorcyclist was a member of an outlaw motorcycle gang with a criminal record. Because he had a criminal record, I had to fingerprint him so that the RCMP records can cancel him out as deceased. I went to the morgue which was full of about ten dead bodies covered in sheets in a very crowded room. It smelled of death. So, I had to check under each sheet to find the dead biker. As I walked around, I accidentally knocked into the charred remains of one of the victims from the plane crash. Some of the charred flesh dropped to the floor. Well, I must say it startled me a bit. Now I had to clean it up and put the charred flesh gently back on the dead body. I eventually found the dead biker.

My training courses came into play here. I had a couple of options opened to me to get good proper fingerprints so that they could be sent back to our HQ's in Ottawa. As rigor mortis had set in, I had to either cut his fingers off, and roll them, or bend them open. This is the last little bit of satisfaction a police officer gets when he gets to deal with a criminal who has given the police a bad time while he was living on this earth. So, with a grin, I broke open his hands, and fingers, and printed them, and said to myself, the rest belongs to the devil

Chapter 13

HUMAN BRAINS SPLATTERED OVER THE WHOLE ROOM

Another educational incident I had to investigate was when a local older man in the Gibson's community was having a difficult time with his wife, who was a bit of a tyrant. He was arrested for impaired driving on Friday night. He was given a promise to appear in court at a later date and released. He decided to get drunk again and was arrested again on Saturday night for impaired driving, and this time he was not released, but remained in jail. He was released from jail on Monday having appeared in front of a Justice of Peace (Magistrate) and made bail.

The next day he got drunk, and a put a shotgun in his mouth, and pulled the trigger. The neighbours heard the shot and called the Detachment. I was to investigate this incident, so I went to the house which was on the main street along the Gibson's waterfront. This house was situated a few houses north of where the movie prop house for the CBC movie series called MOLLY'S REACH. The door was open, there were no lights on, so I walked in. I looked around this very simple cottage style house, and what came next was a shock, and it startled me at first. There in a small front room lay the victim in a chair. The top of his head was blown off, and blood, and brains were splattered all over the wall, and ceiling behind him. The hungry neighbourhood cats followed me into house and started lapping up the remains. I called the Detachment who notified the Coroner's Service who eventually removed the body.

The Detachment commander had another member notify the deceased's wife, who had taken up residence at a different place prior to this and was advised of her husband's demise. What came next was a real eye opener to me. The deceased's wife came over to the house almost immediately, and without any emotion, she chased the cats out, and started to clean up the deceased's remains. I found out later that they were recent immigrants from an eastern European country, possibly Hungary or Romania.

Chapter 14

CUTTING ONE'S PRIVATE PARTS OFF

Another notable incident is worth mentioning - something that would make every male person cringe. One mild winter day, I got a call to attend at a residence where our volunteer ambulance service had just picked up a young male, and were enroute to the Lions Gate Hospital, in North Vancouver. They did not know what happened. When I got to the residence, which looked very much like a shack, I noticed a lot of blood particularly along the snowy path on the property. No one was at the residence, so I opened the door, and I could see a trail of blood. There were a number of cats around, which was very typical of this hippy lifestyle shack. I followed the cats who were going ahead of me on a trail of blood leading outside to a small woodshed. The door was open, so the cats, and I walked in. There on the chopping block I saw what looked like two testicles, and some skin tissue, and a lot of blood. There was also a pair of scissors on the chopping block.

I called the Detachment who then advised me that they had just received a call from the ambulance service informing them, that the victim told them that he had cut his own testicles off with the scissors. AM I TO GATHER EVIDENCE??? YOU GOTTA TO BE KIDDING. As this was not a criminal offence, but a self-mutilation case, the detachment commander said it was not necessary to seize anything from the scene. So, I left the cats to take charge of whatever cleanup was required, (the cats are pretty good in this department).

I went back to the shack, and searched for other evidence such as drugs, identification, etc. I found that his girlfriend lived in another shack not far from where he lived. I found her in her shack. I told her of what happened to her boyfriend, and she said she was not surprised. Then she said that a few days prior they had had a meal together where out of the blue, and with no explanation, he had stood up, took out his penis, and pissed on the food. She said he was hooked on some drugs, which could be, LSD, marihuana, and combinations of other chemicals that altered his proper brain function. I concluded my file on this matter and carried on.

It was several months later that this individual was walking around the BC Ferry Terminal at Horseshoe Bay when he noticed me standing outside my police car waiting for the ferry to arrive. He approached me, and we had a brief conversation. He said he was in a recovery program from narcotics and had recovered from his self-mutilation incident. I wished him well, and we boarded the ferry. I was never to see him again. I often wondered how he functioned later in his life.

My time in Gibson's, was when the hippy lifestyle took to the mainstream. As a young man, and a police officer with a very short haircut, I pretty much stood out. During my many evening patrols I encountered a lot of abuse of who I was and was called a lot of offending names. I learned to brush it off until the right moment came when the offender who abused me was in a situation in violation of the law. Well, I was now able to settle the score. I was in top physical condition, so it served me to my benefit.

Chapter 15

MEETING JONI MITCHELL/
MEETING MY WIFE CAROLINE

For one brief moment during my time in Gibson's, I had chance meeting with a celebrity. I was in the courtroom waiting to give evidence on a traffic ticket offence and there was a young woman waiting to contest her traffic ticket for driving her 450 SL Mercedes Benz into a ditch one raining night and was ticketed (for driving with undue care & attention). She got talking to another couple that was there on another matter, and eventually they recognized her as being the famous Canadian folk singer, Joni MITCHELL. We all introduced ourselves to each other. I didn't say much to Joni at that time, but the older couple said that their daughter would have liked to have met her etc. When I left the courtroom, Joni having dealt with her case, followed me out. I started to walk to my car when Joni called out to me. I walked back to her, and she asked if I would like to join her for a dinner date. I said it would be nice as there were not too many single women around Gibson's. She told me to call her at the Lord Jim's Lodge where she was staying.

I called her a few days later and met her at the Lodge. When I got there, I found her in the lobby talking to a couple of hippy guys, who were really trying to sell her on their new invention of a guitar. Joni said hi to me and said she would be a couple of minutes. Well, I waited and waited, but these hippy guys would not let her go. I thought that I may have gotten the date wrong or was being stood up or as these guys probably thought, Joni could not possibly be wanting to see a short haired cop like me. So, I got up and was about to leave, when Joni ran up to me and grabbed my arm and asked to me to wait.

She told these hippy guys, she would think about the guitar. They left disappointed. She turned her attention to me and hugged me tightly and told me she just could not get rid of these guys. She also commented that her being a hippy and me a cop was a bit unusual in the hippy world, but she liked me and wanted to see me.

We went into dining room had a wonderful dinner, which I paid for. After dinner she wanted to show me her stone house that she was having built on her ten acre waterfront property near the Lord Jim's Lodge. She showed me around and proceeded to play some of her songs. I got to say I was very impressed. I had not been a fan of her folk music, actually I was not a follower of any music. This was a new experience, and I was being entertained by a bigtime star.

We talked about her life and our common roots, her being from Saskatoon, Sask. She was married and now divorced from a well-known musical talent, last name Mitchell. She lived in California most of the time, but liked her place in B.C. I drove her back to the Lodge, and she did not want me to go home, and insisted that I stay the night. We were twenty-year olds from Saskatchewan just having fun. She wanted to see me again and we had another date.

I met Joni at the Lord Jim's lodge, and we had dinner. This time she said that she wanted to spend a night in her new house as she had not slept there before and was a bit scared to be alone. She wanted it to be special. Again, she played her songs and played some of her new songs that she was going to record in California in a couple of months. She said she was getting prepared to go on singing tour and was hoping that I could come along, perhaps change my job, and be part of her music support group. I said I was pretty much committed at that time to the RCMP, but we could keep in contact. She said that she truly wanted to see me when she returned from her singing tour. I said I would contact her. I stood guard that night like a good Mountie, while Joni slept.

Several months later, I did go to her place and the Lodge, and left messages with her watchman on her property to contact me. I never heard from her again. I was puzzled as she did seem sincere in wanting to see more of me. It could be her hippy lifestyle where drugs were paramount, and where one loses some reality or, it might have been possible that she may have tried to call me during my undercover duty days, and was told like other friends, that I was on an assignment, and could not be contacted. I basically disappeared. It was not meant to be. Furthermore, Joni had a smoking habit that personally bothered me, but I tolerated it at the time. However, I believe I would have not convinced her to give up her desire for smoking. Truly I was too straightlaced for her lifestyle. I knew Joni had a child and kept it a secret until now. I was glad to hear that she managed to meet up with her daughter, who also had a child years later, and was now a proud grandmother. She has suffered with some personal health issues (brain aneurysm) in her senior years. I wish her well and best of health with all that is going on in her life.

AT THE SAME TIME AND FAST FORWARD

IN THE SUMMER OF 1983, I went to a house party in North Vancouver with Jacqueline, my date at the time. At the party I met a very beautiful woman who was there with her date. There was an immediate attraction. As the evening progressed, I asked her to dance and I told her where I worked, and said if it was possible, she could call me, as exchanging phone numbers at the party could be life threatening.

Two weeks after this party I got a call from Jacqueline's mother saying Jackie had died from a brain aneurysm and she was calling all Jackie's friends to a small WAKE, and just to share their thoughts, etc.

It was about three or four months later, that I received a call at the Burnaby RCMP Detachment from a woman named Caroline who wanted me to call her. At first, I could not recall who she was, but after some explanation on Caroline's part saying that we met at house party in North Vancouver, where I was with my date named Jackie. She was informed by the hostess of this party that Jackie had died and said if Caroline was still interested, she should call me. Caroline eventually got up the courage and called me.

After a series of phone calls and date's, I found out that Caroline was a widow with two daughters, Samantha age seventeen, and Vanessa age thirteen. In 1971, when Joni and I met, Caroline and her husband, Michael were celebrating the birth of their daughter Vanessa in Calcutta, India. Caroline's husband, Michael died in India 6 years prior to us meeting at the North Vancouver party.

Caroline told me that she had just gone through some legal proceedings surrounding Michael and his first wife's children from India, who were after their share of the properties in Canada that were in their father's name, to which they felt they were entitled to. She said that Michael was killed in a car crash and had died from head trauma.

Caroline and I got married in 1985 and went on several trips to the UK to visit her relatives and friends. It was during a visit at one of her friend's places, where the host told me that Michael was murdered in India for having an affair with another woman. The woman's brother did not like Michael and threw him over the apartment balcony. Michael died from severe head trauma. There was no police investigation into the matter.

I now have five step grandchildren. Samantha 's children, Ethan Whiting, Sebastian Whiting, Kieran Whiting. Vanessa's children, Cole Andruik and Alexis Andruik. Caroline and I are still married.

It is a strange coincidence that the year of 1971 and the brain aneurysm, are these two events in my life that would be connected to meeting Caroline and eventually Joni having a brain aneurysm later in her life.

I later found a Coroner's report from India in Caroline's paper documents, stating that Michael died from severe head trauma. There was no mention of how he got this head trauma, and no mention of a car accident. Caroline was told by the Indian Coroner at the time that Michael's condition was similar to someone who was involved in a car accident. I guess Caroline, through shock and confusion at the time accepted that Michael had been killed in a car crash.

My experience in dealing with the Indian Justice System during my part in the 1985 AIR INDIA PLANE BOMBING INVESTIGATIONS, was that they are not necessarily correct and police investigations are done differently there, than what we in Canada accept as credible. In this case it can be compared to the American baseball game, which is STRIKE THREE AND YOU ARE OUT.

Chapter 16

GETTING BEATEN UP BY AN OUTLAW MOTORCYCLE GANG

I had been in Gibson's for about a year, and was wanting a transfer; however, it was still pretty exciting police work. The detachment got pretty busy, so an additional two constables were transferred in. I was on patrol one evening with a Cst. Robert KENNEDY, who grew up in a quiet place in Nova Scotia. He was a bit short in height, and overweight in stature.

One evening we went to do a bar check at the Peninsula Hotel. Well, one biker from the 101 Knights outlaw motorcycle club, (later incorporated into the Hells Angels Motorcycle Club) named MUNROE, jumped up, and hit me with his fist. I grabbed him by his throat, and jacket, and told him that he was under arrest for assaulting a peace officer and proceeded to drag him out of the bar. He put up a hell of a fight, but I quickly got him out the door, and told Cst. KENNEDY to hold the door shut so I could get MUNROE into the police car. Well KENNEDY was not very strong, and a bit of a coward. Just then a bunch of the bikers pushed the door open and came charging at me. The battle was on as I tried my best to hang on to MUNROE. There were fists flying at my face and body. I took a real beating. They grabbed MUNROE from me and went back into the bar.

I later found Cst. KENNEDY hiding behind the barroom door. I told him to get into the police car, and off we went to the Detachment. I got the NCO i/c, Cpl. Lou BIGGEMAN out of bed, and we called Cst. Don BROST to come into the Detachment. We grabbed a shotgun, and a .308 rifle, ammo, got into two police cars, and drove to the Pen Hotel. MUNROE had already taken off with some of his biker buddies. The corporal advised some of the bikers that we would eventually deal with MUNROE.

The deal was a bit unorthodox. I was to meet MUNROE the next day around 3 pm behind the Bank of Montreal in the parking lot away from the public and we would battle it out. I went the next day to the meeting spot, and MUNROE was a "no show". I went looking for him in town and found him near the liquor store shopping centre parking lot. I approached him, maybe in a bit of an aggressive manner and asked him how come he did not show up for our battle. He quickly said that I did a number on him in that fight last night, and that he did not ever want to fight me again. He stayed true to his word for the remainder of my time in Gibson's. I stopped him and harassed him as often as I could (quite acceptable in those days), and he was polite, and cooperated every time. He looked kind of funny, portraying a tough guy image in his 5'5" small body, trying to stand tall. He had dirty long red hair, and stinky biker clothes, rode his big Harley Davidson with raised handlebars, roaring around Gibson's.

After about a year, and half in Gibson's the RCMP decided to transfer me to the Powell River Detachment. It was a larger Detachment of which I do not recall experiencing any earthshattering incidents. I had more of a social life there, as there were more members at the detachment. I had regular shifts, and there were more available females around. I did meet my first wife, Lori there. She was of Italian heritage, so I got into the whole Italian lifestyle of pasta, and wine cuisine.

Our staffing section were looking for members who had some accounting experience, or a university degree in Commerce to join their newly formed Commercial Crime Section. The S/Sgt in charge of the Powell River Detachment was a former RCMP Drug Squad N.C.O., so when I went to Vancouver to meet with our Staffing Section in hopes of getting on the Commercial Crime Section, I was directed to the Drug Section. I met with the Officer In Charge (O.I.C.) of the Vancouver Drug Section who was an Inspector. He advised me that my S/Sgt felt that I would be a good candidate for undercover work. He asked me a bunch of questions and said he would get back to me on whether he wanted me on his unit. I drove back to Powell River, and within a week my S/Sgt. told me to get my outstanding files in order and not to talk to anybody as to where I was being transferred. I was to ship out within a week. Everybody within the Detachment and some civilian friends were quite taken back, but I said I could not talk about it. Everything was to be top secret. I just disappeared.

Chapter 17

UNDERCOVER NARCOTICS AGENT

I packed my belongings and drove to Vancouver. My instructions were that, as soon as I got to Horseshoe Bay, I was to call a phone number, and I would be given my instructions as to where I was to go. My new bosses/handlers were Sgt. Karl RICHERT, and Constable John PATTERSON, and they had a hotel room picked out, and I was to go there. They said they would see me the following morning and set things in motion.

I settled in for the night, and early next morning they came to my hotel room, and I was given a briefing on what I was going to be involved in. They told me that they usually send members on an undercover course, but they had no time to arrange that, so it was "On The Job Training". They told me that the RCMP never lost an undercover agent, and if it was me, then I was the first. They tried to prepare me with some of the jargon used by the drug underworld, and what I had to watch out for. I now was given the opportunity to change my name and have a whole new identity. My handlers said I looked Italian and resembled an Italian drug dealer in the Toronto area. We settled on the name of Antonio

Joseph VALLANTINI, in short Tony VALLANTINI. I also got a driver's licence with my new name.

In the meantime, which was for about a month I went shopping for an apartment with RICHERT and PATTERSON. They picked out a one bedroom apartment on the top floor of an apartment building that was pretty secure which was situated on the corner of 14th Ave., and Burrard St., VANCOUVER. It was a couple blocks from where RICHERT was living, which was great if I had some unexpected visitors. We rented some basic furniture from a furniture company. I was on an expense account, and all my living arrangements were paid by the RCMP, so I was able to bank my small paycheques.

I decided to sell my Dodge Demon car to a friend in Gibson's and purchased an older model Volkswagon Bug to run around in Vancouver. I was given a mug shot book and dossiers on various drug users, dealers, and traffickers in the Vancouver area, and I was to memorize them should I encounter them in my under-cover work.

During my training in Depot Division, one of the classes that I did extremely well in was in memory and observation, which was a definite asset in this line of work.

We waited for my beard to grow, which was a new experience as I was always clean shaven. My hair was taking its time to grow long, so we decided that I purchase a wig, which looked realistic if I was going start my street drug purchases. During my "get ready period ", I decided to join a karate class to stay in shape. This was good in one sense; however, drug addicts were out of shape, and sickly looking. I had to portray an image of a drug addict, so I put together whatever skills I possessed trying to look sickly and hit the streets.

My first drug deal was from a individual, who I vaguely remem-ber meeting sometime before I embarked on this eventful time of my life, but could not place him as to where it was at that moment. I was told that this man was in the lounge at the Sheraton Hotel, and it would be reasonably safe to engage him in a conversation relating to purchase of drugs. My handlers showed me a picture of this person and described how he usually dressed, like in a jean jacket. The jean jacket was quite common amongst most of the low-level drug underworld that worked the streets at that time. They are creatures of habit, as I later found out, they maintained their usual daily dress code, and if you got close enough to them, you could smell them - hygiene was not their top priority. They usually did not change their clothes for quite some time. This made it a lot easier for drug users, who usually recognize drug dealers, by the way dealers dressed, wore their beard or goatee, so forth. Drug users shared information with other drug users about the best drugs for the money from the various drug dealers on the street.

Sure enough, I spotted this guy and casually walked over to him and addressed him by his street name. As one would expect he looked surprised, and tried to brush me off, but I sat down in a chair next to him and started my BS about getting his name from others on the street and I told him I was in the same business as him. He looked surprised and said he did not know what I was talking about. I offered to buy him a drink, and he accepted. Everybody likes to get a free drink, especially when it was on government expense, and I drank a lot of booze on the taxpayer's expense during my undercover operation. After a short conversation about nothing important, I suggested that we get down to business as we were all out to make money. I said I would be interested in purchasing a small amount of stuff (which was the street jargon for heroin), and if it was as good as my friends said, then I would be prepared to purchase larger amounts. He quizzed me on who I was, and I laid on a lot of my bogus business dealings. After about forty-five minutes to an hour of this, he asked me to come with him for a ride. I thought this was OK; however, my handlers later told me that I was putting myself in danger as they may not be able to protect me. I never did that again.

We drove around the neighbourhood for about fifteen minutes, and I could see him checking his rear-view mirror. He told me he was checking for tail (term used by the drug underworld to see if they are being followed), as he felt that I was being watched. I told him he had nothing to worry about, as I was being careful in not getting caught by the narcs (a term used by the underworld for drug enforcement police). Eventually he pulled over not far from the Sheraton Hotel and said he would take a chance on me. He handed me a small bundle of heroin in a balloon, and said it was good stuff and we could do a future deal. I paid him for the drugs and left his car. He took off, and I continued walking until I was picked up by my handlers. We went over my first drug deal of what I did OK, or maybe passable, and what I should do in the future.

My handlers took off for their homes while I stayed up into early morning hours to make my notes in absolute detail. This would prove to be a great benefit to me in the future, as I was going to have to testify in court sometime within a one-to-three year period. It depended on the crown/defence maneuvers which happened quite often during that time. I would have to remember what the person looked like and most important was what they said on whether or not I engaged them to committing a drug transaction for which they did not wish. This was called "entrapment", a term used quite often by defence lawyers. Sometimes, this was a bit of a challenge as I was pretty much drunk most of the time, and the defence lawyers tried to make that a big issue. It did not work, as the judge gave me the benefit of the doubt, and the drug dealers got convicted.

The next drug transaction was a small street purchase from a street drug pusher, accomplished by me engaging in conversation with some drug addicts. It was a fast easy purchase for a small amount of heroin. My handlers later identified the drug dealer, then it was the usual routine of back to my apartment to make detailed notes.

The next day it was a drug deal that was slightly different. I was to meet with a big balding, truck driving looking man, who had a big beard, and his partner, who was a slight, smaller man. Again, it took a bit of bravery on my part to approach strangers who were not receptive, but I knew I had to hook up with them to purchase the heroin. I worked up my courage, and with the offer to buy them drinks, things moved along in my favour.

My handlers suggested that I make another simple street purchase, which was successful. Then I was to repeat contacting the two previous two higher level drug dealers, which went rather smoothly with a lot less conversation in the purchase of a sizeable amount of heroin. A few days later I was to find out from my handlers of my second to last purchase from the big balding guy and his partner. Then this all amounted to a frightening, yet memorable experience in my undercover training period.

My handlers had previously warned me to be aware of my surrounding, and to be vigilant of suspect people who may have me followed by someone in their organization. They also told me that should I get ripped off on a drug deal, I was to threaten them that I would kill them, and I would have to seriously portray my intentions to them. I was to convince them that I would carry out this act, and that I was serious in my business. There was the usual threat where drug dealers were out to avoid being caught and were determined to cause serious harm to the undercover operator which could result in the undercover operator's death. My handlers told me that they have never lost an undercover agent; however, if it happened to me, they said, I would be the first to lose my life in a drug operation. I assumed that since they were my handlers and bodyguards, so to speak, that when I was picked up by them, and driven back to my apartment in their car, that they would look after my safety. That was definitely not the case in this particular situation.

We arrived at my apartment in pretty quickly, and my handlers/bodyguards quickly hit my beer stocked fridge and grabbed a cold one. I got a cold beer, and we just stood there drinking beer in the galley kitchen and dining room. About fifteen minutes passed, and there was an unexpected knock on the door. This was unusual as this was a secret hideout, and only the three us knew about it. They told me to answer the door.

I opened the door and then I got a SURPRISE. I was now facing the three guys from whom I had purchased heroin. First at the door was the guy I recognized from a year or so before, but could not place him as to where that was at the moment. He was the one I met at the Sheraton Hotel, and behind him was the slight smaller partner of the big balding guy, who then brought up the rear. The first guy looked at me and said, "Tony we want to talk to you".

He started to push his way into my apartment, which I was going to defend to the end. In my micro mille second response, I went into my karate/street fighting stance. I grabbed the first guy by the throat with my right hand, and with lightning/frightful manoeuvre I swung my left arm around his neck. My intent at that time was to break his neck swiftly, which I felt quite capable of doing and if that happened, I would have regretted it to this day, because I would have killed him. Then I would quickly knock the smaller man aside gasping for air as I punched him in the solar plexus, and a knife swipe to his throat. The next guy was going to be a big problem for me, and I felt somewhat briefly defeated, with no game plan of how I was going to stop them from coming into my apartment. As I had that guy in a head lock, my handlers immediately jumped into action. They quickly grabbed me off him and told me that these were the members from our drug squad. I had a rather quick adrenaline melt down, as you could imagine at that moment. We shared many laughs about this incident throughout our careers. Doug, the guy I had in a head lock encountered colon cancer later in his life. The cancer eventually won the battle, and he now rests in well - deserved peace.

They wanted to see how I would perform under strenuous conditions, and with questioning by the drug dealers. They said I met their expectations, and it was now time for a little celebration. I got pretty drunk with a lot of the other members of the drug squad, who came in later on. They gave me the next day off to sober up.

Chapter 18

MY FIRST NARCOTIC PURCHASES AND LIFE ON THE STREET

I made several small-time drug purchases of heroin, which I found pretty easy to make. I seemed to blend in OK, and a lot of times I put on the act of being sick, which was the usual appearance of most addicts. I became friends with a young Native Indian woman, Christine NAVATRAL, who was an addict, and supported her drug habit by being a prostitute. She was a pleasant woman approximately twenty years old, and I felt sorry for her that she had gotten into this racket. Her boyfriend was a notorious new immigrant from Czechoslovakia, a communist country at the time, and part of the Soviet Union. He was part of a group of immigrants that our Liberal Government of the day decided to let in, who eventually became criminals, or they may have been criminals in their own country prior to coming to Canada. She helped me make some connections with drug pushers, one of whom was her boyfriend. I got her to sign my arm cast which I used as a prop-drug addicts / pushers would not suspect me as an undercover cop with a broken arm. I still have that prop hanging in my garage, with her name faintly signed on it.

Upon the completion of my operation, her boyfriend was arrested, and was shown a picture of me, as to whom he sold heroin to. He was charged with trafficking in heroin. Shortly thereafter, Christine mysteriously turned up dead from an overdose of heroin. Vancouver City Police investigated the crime but did not have enough evidence to charge him for murder in her death. He was the most likely suspect in her death. I am sure (or I hoped) he met with a violent end.

There was another female drug addict who at times was reasonably attractive. She was an American from California. Whenever she saw me in the bar, she always came over, and I would buy her a drink. She tried very hard to get me to take her home with me and told me she wanted to have sex with me. I always made an excuse that I had someone waiting for me. She said that did not bother her, she just wanted to have sex with me, anywhere, anyplace, which was quite common during that hippy period. I continued to tell her I may consider it sometime later, but I needed to get some heroin for me, and my girlfriend (a totally made-up story) who was waiting at home for me. She always tried to kiss me, and I tried to avoid it most times, as you never knew where those lips were most recently (US President, Wild Willie Billie Clinton was not the only one getting it). I often wondered if she became a victim of a drug overdose, or murder. Other than her drug dependency, she seemed like a nice person, unfortunately she was wasting her life away.

There was a time that some Vancouver City Police Drug Squad members knew that I was an undercover RCMP member, so they decided to make things look a little more authentic. A couple of detectives (one who was a former member of the RCMP now with VPD, and who had died a few years ago of this writing) jumped me on the street and engaged me in a major physical fight with them. One of the detectives punched me hard in the stomach.

It looked good from the enforcement perspective, as the drug dealers who were witness to this street fight, and who may have had suspicions of me, now knew I was not a cop, as cops don't usually beat up on other cops. I got scratches, and bruises, and was arrested, and thrown into their police car, then transported to the VPD solitary jail cell at the Vancouver Police Station for about an hour. It was a terrible experience, but I now know what a prisoner in similar circumstances feels like when they're confined in a small dark room with no light, and very little air. I was eventually let out of solitary confinement and put into holding cell with about twelve other inmates, filled with foul body odour. Everybody asked everybody else what they were in for. I told them that I was in for drug trafficking, and possession. There were no murderers in the group which was a bit of a relief. One of the inmates who said he was in for drug trafficking, seemed to be a bit scared of the other inmates, so he started up a conversation with me. He said that they usually gave you methadone for your heroin habit, and he was going to ask for a lot of methadone. I said I was going to see what transpired.

A short time later a guard came in and told me that I was to be transferred to New Westminster police cells for an outstanding warrant, and that was just the same for this friendly drug dealer. We were then served a lunch. It was a very basic meal, and far from being appetizing. Sure enough just as we finished this amazing five-star restaurant food, (yeah, sure, it was, a slice of bread, some mashed potatoes), we were hand cuffed and escorted to a police van that was to transport us to the New Westminster police Cells.

I did not know how long I was going to keep this up, as I was not a drug user and was not going to take methadone. So, I silently prayed to the Good Lord Jesus, my Saviour, and asked for a miracle, which arrived when our police van en route to New Westminster came to a sudden stop. The police constable told me to get out of the van as the Mounties had further dealings in store for me. I said my goodbyes to my friendly drug user, who asked if he could have my methadone share. I said if they handed it out, he was welcomed to it. I never saw him again. My drug squad handlers came to the rescue. They threw me into the back of their vehicle, and we took off. They were laughing like hell when I told them of my three to four hours of incarceration. You see, there is a God.

My handlers decided it was time for me to engage in meeting with the higher level of drug traffickers. We rented a 1973 Oldsmobile Toronado. It was a really flashy car, and it would be part of my persona, portraying me to be a successful drug dealer. I was now sporting a mustache and goatee, and looked the part of a tough, gruff looking Italian man. I had a driver's licence in my undercover name of Antonio Joseph VALENTINI, born in the Toronto area. I dressed the part - platform shoes, bell bottom pants, which were the some of the most uncomfortable clothing of that hippy era. Oh yes, I forgot to mention, I was a non-smoker, so I had to master the style of being a seasoned smoker and did not cough when I inhaled. I am sure it was a bit of a laughable sight for some of the seasoned smoking drug squad members, who'd just met me, but I took it in good fun, and carried on.

Chapter 19

MEETING ONE OF CANADA'S LAST MEN SENTENCED TO HANG

One interesting incident was when I was introduced to an older woman who I believe was in her early senior years. This was one of my first ventures in meeting with a higher-level drug dealer. Apparently, she had kept in contact with an old boyfriend of hers, who back in the late 1950's, or early 1960's was sentenced to DEATH BY HANGING for a murder he was involved with. His death sentence was later commuted to life in prison, and he'd spent several years in prison. He had been released on full parole, then got in contact with his old girlfriend. She found out that he still had the criminal element in him, only now he was trafficking in heroin. This disturbed her, as she had grandchildren, and she felt he was contributing to the increasing narcotic problem with the younger generation, so she was compelled to remove his element off the street. She contacted our drug squad, who arranged for my handlers, and me to meet with her. We got our storyline down, and the description, habits, etc., of her boyfriend. He would be about my Grand-fathers age at the time, and he always dressed in a suit, sometimes in a topcoat, and always wore a hat. He reminded me of someone still stuck in the 1940's era.

This man hung out in the Blackstone Hotel Lounge on Granville Street in Vancouver and was easy to spot. I found him sitting to one side of the Lounge. Sure enough, there he was, dressed in a dark suit, glasses, hat on his head, and he was smoking. I approached him and started the conversation that I thought he dressed like an important gentleman. He smiled, and I asked him if l could join him. He pointed to the chair across from him. I sat down, and ordered a drink, and got him one as well. We talked about life in general, and then I got into the conversation that I was in various businesses, and they made me some money. Eventually the conversation turned to narcotics, and he became more interested. He agreed to sell me some heroin, and few months later when my undercover operation was over, he found out who I was, and he was on his way back to jail. I felt kind of sad for him. He got away from the noose around his neck, and he would have been one of the last ones to be hung by the Canadian courts. Now he would be spending his final days of his life in the crowbar hotel. It was unfortunate that he decided to make some money selling drugs.

Chapter 20

ALMOST CHOKED THE DRUG TRAFFICKER TO DEATH

My handlers got another lead from one of our drug member's informants. It was agreed that I would meet with the informant and get a storyline that we both could agree on. Furthermore, the informant's wife may accompany him on some of the transactions, so I had to have all the B.S. in order. She accepted it, and did not know who I really was, so things moved along. I met some of his drug dealers and made some small purchases from the informant's acquaintances.

At one point I got introduced to a small - time drug dealer. We agreed to do a deal, but he wanted the money up front. After some lengthy conversation I agreed to front him half of the money for the purchase. He took the money and told me where to meet him in the late evening hours and promised me he would have the drugs. I felt that I may have got ripped off; however, I went to the meeting spot which was somewhere on Beach Ave., in Vancouver. I waited in the dark, and sure enough he showed up, and got into the rear seat of my car. He gave me a sob story that he could not get the drugs for me. I said I wanted my money back. He said he did not have it, as he gave it to another dealer to purchase the heroin, and subsequently got ripped off as well.

Well, I got mad, and grabbed him by the throat, and threatened him that I was going to kill him, because he ripped me off. I put my arm around his neck and started to strangle him. He started screaming that he did not want to die. I punched him a couple of times and kept on choking him. I said (with a lot of profanity) that I wanted my money back. All of sudden there was a foul smell in the car. He lost control of his bowels in his pants.

As my car was bugged/wired, this was all being played out in my handler's car. My handlers heard what was going on, and told me later, that they actually thought that I might kill the guy in the process. However, I let go of the guy, and told him to get out of the car, and that if I saw him again, I would settle the score. My handlers heard what transpired, and John (one of my handlers decided to follow this guy on foot. John said that this guy ran through the lobby of an apartment building that he had access to and ran through towards the back door, and down the back lane so fast that he could not catch him. I never saw that guy again, and basically lost the money, which was a small amount. It was a well learned lesson. I apologize to the Canadian taxpayers for the loss of the money.

So, it was back to my apartment to make my notes. My handlers invited a few other Drug Squad members, which happened on several occasions, which also included Constable Larry CAMPBELL. My apartment was basically a meeting place for the drug squad street crew, and also an opportunity for me to meet with some of our enforcement personnel. We would drink a lot of beer, which I always seemed to end up paying for. Because I was on an expense account, and banking my pay cheques, some members took advantage of me, by not paying the price my handlers set for the beer sales. Some of the "cheapoos cops" felt I should pay for the beer and put up with the inconvenience of having them party at my apartment. This was beneficial should I encounter them on the street during my operation, as well as them knowing who I was.

CAMPBELL resigned from the RCMP shortly thereafter and became an Assistant Coroner for the Province of B.C., and later chief coroner. He later became the mayor of Vancouver. He was a bit outspoken and his popularity of being mayor was starting to decline. He made a comment about the then Reform/ Conservative party leader, Preston MANNING of being a "moron". The Liberal prime minster at the time, Paul MARTIN, thought they needed a senator from the west who was more left leaning, and not afraid to speak his mind, so he appointed Larry to the Canadian Senate, and a pay cheque for life. Larry and I had met at two casual functions over the years while he was a mayor, and once while he was a senator.

Chapter 21

MEETING A CRAZY ESCAPEE FROM THE BC PENITENTIARY

As part of my undercover operation, I used to frequent all the nightclubs in the Vancouver area, like the Penthouse, owned by an Canadian / Italian family. There was another strip nightclub called the "Zanzibar". I got friendly with a few of the strippers and bought them a lot of drinks. They knew I was in the drug business and helped me out by getting me lined up to purchase some heroin from their drug pusher friends. On one such an occasion I met an older man, wearing a suit jacket, and he also wore a hat. We got talking, and he told me that he escaped from the B.C. Penitentiary. I could not recall what he was in for, but it had to be a serious offence if he was in the B.C. Pen. He took a handkerchief out from the inside breast pocket of his jacket, and opened it up, and in the handkerchief was an older model .45 cal. revolver. It was loaded. He said he was not going back to jail and was prepared to shoot it out with the police should they confront him. I felt he was a bit crazy, but he said he could help me out in getting me hooked up with a drug dealer. He told me to meet him the next day in his apartment which he shared with one of the younger strippers.

The next day, I went to his apartment in the west end of Vancouver. I knocked on the door. I heard a voice coming from within the apartment telling me to come in. I pushed the door open and saw that the room was in total darkness. The voice said to go over to a chair under that black light, which was the only stark lighting in the room. I went and sat down, knowing full well this was a crazy guy with a loaded gun, and an escapee from the B.C. Pen, who told me he was not going to be taken back there alive. He started interrogating me on what kind of a business I was in, as he felt he was not sure of who I was and was not able to trust me. I kept my cool and answered his questions. His interrogation went on for a little while. There was a period of no conversation where he obviously was watching to see how I reacted, or was I being nervous in this environment. Then I was able to see where he was sitting in the darken room, as his cigarette smoke came flowing out. I looked towards the direction of the cigarette smoke, and said I had had enough of this BS, and let's go, and get some drinks. He said, "OK", and off we went in my big Oldsmobile Toronado to see his girlfriend stripping away at Club Zanzibar. She was young enough to be his daughter, I had to assure him that I enjoyed her show, and in fact she was a good performer. He then made a couple of calls and set me up with a guy named "Tiny", who later came to the club. Well, "Tiny" was not a small man by any means, but a 300+ lbs, six foot man. I bought the drinks, and we got along OK.

Tiny was willing to do the deal with me and told me where we could meet the next day. Everything went according to plan. I said that I would like to do another deal with him if his stuff was OK. He assured me that his heroin was of good quality. I was able to do another deal with Tiny without the intervention of the BC Pen Escapee a few weeks later.

It was sometime later upon the completion of my undercover operation that my handlers told me that the BC Pen escapee had been arrested without any shootout by the Vancouver Police Department. They chose not to tell me, as this would be beneficial for my safety. Should I be confronted by the underworld drug dealers about "the escapee's arrest", I would be just as surprised as anyone would be upon hearing the news of his arrest. Things can get pretty dangerous when those people you're dealing with, who have killed, or arranged for certain people to get killed, if it had an impact on dealer's livelihood.

Chapter 22

ON A HUNT FOR UZI SUBMACHINE GUNS/MACHINE PISTOLS

Our street intelligence members got some information that some of the underworld figures were in possession of an Israeli military assault machine gun called an "Uzi", and / or machine pistols. This was a very effective weapon that their troops used during their " Seven-Day War ".

In any event, I was to try to obtain whatever information from my contacts in the underworld and offer to purchase it at whatever reasonable cost. Well, my cover team had come up with a story that I had a contact in one of the American Army Bases that could supply me with a throw away small 9 mm pistols.

To secure that story, my cover team, and I were invited by our American DEA liaison officer, Dick TEEFEE (phonetic) to meet at the Fort Hood Military Base in Washington state. The DEA also supplied me with an American social insurance identity card. The Colonel in charge of the Fort Hood Army headquarters was very hospitable, and welcomed us, a typical example of all the Americans that I have met. He showed us around the base, and we got to see the cadets in various stages of their training. One impressive piece of military vehicles he showed us was a Hugh Army Tank that had been damaged in the "Seven Day War ", and that was in for repairs. He showed me where their gunsmiths prepared all their weapons for military campaigns. A sergeant showed me how to disassemble a 9 mm pistol.

Part of my undercover story line was that I had a relative working at this base, and at various times he would take parts of the pistols out of the base, and they would later be assembled at home to be sold to the underworld for their hits (killing of their rivals), and the gun could not be traced as there were no serial numbers. We were then treated to a delicious mess lunch at the base. Later that evening the DEA, and U.S. Customs agents entertained us to no end with all the nightclubbing, etc.

I was the more sober one of our team as I had a lot of things to absorb and write my notes when I got back to Canada. Well, I piled Sgt. Karl RICHERT in the back seat of the Mustang and put Cst. Gary KILGORE in the front passenger seat and drove to Canada. I passed many state troopers who had vehicles pulled over along I-5. It was a long ride home, so I was picking up speed, which eventually was not the right decision. A state trooper pulled me over somewhere between Bellingham and Blaine. I had to wake up my drunk cover guys, who explained to the state trooper that we were on a business trip with the DEA, and we would pay the ticket. The state trooper told me he would normally have me arrested, but under the circumstances told me to slow down, and get across the border. My cover guys later sent the state of Washington some money.

I was relieved to be back in Canada. I eventually met up with an American drug dealer, named Mike, who had been busted for possessing a pound of heroin, at the Blaine Border Crossing by the US border guards. He was subsequently turned over to the DEA. They found out that Mike purchased the heroin from a drug supplier, named Victor HANSEN, who lived in Burnaby, B.C., and who was doing a rather lucrative business. Mike did not want to go to jail for a long time, so he decided to offer his services to the DEA. The sentences for the USA Drug Enforcement offences are much more, lengthy compared to those of the Canadian Justice system. Mike was prepared to introduce me to Victor, and if we were successful in purchasing some heroin from him, the DEA was prepared to have Mike's charges withdrawn, and we could take down a significant drug dealer.

My drug handlers had set up Mike in an apartment not far from my apartment building. For security reasons I never did let Mike know where I lived. We became friends in the drug business, but where I lived was private. Mike and I socialized together to get to know each other better, so we could really look like we were good friends amongst the drug dealers, and their friends. We went to night clubs that were really strip joints, and I bought the drinks, and dinners on government expense, (I am forever thankful to the Canadian government for having booze on taxpayers' money). Mike was a card dealer at the Tropicana Hotel & Casino in Las Vegas, before he got busted. So, I would go to Mike's apartment, and spend some time waiting for the opportunity to meet up with Victor HANSEN.

In the meantime, he taught me some poker games. He told me to sit down in any position at a pretend table for a game of five-card stud, and he would deal me a royal flush. I was not a gambler nor a card player, but I watched him, and I could not figure out how he was able to deal me a royal flush, and other various card winning hands. He further impressed me with various other card playing hands, such as three of a kind, three aces, etc. He was able to read the cards in other players hands, and told me he was a card counter, a skill required for his job at the Tropicana. He also told me that the DICE GAMES were rigged in favour of the gambling establishment, so the odds of you winning were next to none.

There was talk amongst some of the drug traffickers that there was an undercover agent working the streets, and they'd basically put out a "CONTRACT HIT" for anyone to kill him. There were some intense moments as I did not know who suspected me to be the undercover agent and end my exceptional exciting life. I kept my cool, and relied on my nerves of steel, and kept drinking away the taxpayer's money in the nightclubs. I was amazed that the very guys that were talking about this to me, did not know the guy they wanted killed, was the very guy they were talking to. "Those were the days my friends, they thought they would never end, but they did".

Mike and I would go to the nightclubs on a regular basis and meet up with some of the potential suspects. On one occasion we encountered a drug dealer by the name of Eddie SENGER. Eddie was a big-time dealer, and a very confronting figure. He threw a lot of money around, and let everybody know he was big time player, and a force to be reckoned with.

One evening Mike, and I were in the Penthouse Strip Club enjoying the strip show. We were joined by other drug dealers, and a few show girls. Out of the blue, Eddie approached Mike, and stood next to him. He put his hand in his pocket and took out a huge wad of hundred-dollar bills and started to count.

He got past $2000 - a lot of money at that time - then looked at Mike, and said something to the effect of. "All right, you said you are a big-time dealer in Las Vegas, let's go for the big game."

Mike had started to say something to stall him, and that he wasn't prepared for any card game at that time.

One of the drug dealers, who was known as "The Patch", (he had a patch on one of his eyes, an injury he got in a previous incident having been shot with a shotgun), leaned over to me, and asked where I had met Mike. I told "The Patch" that I had met Mike at the Tropicana Casino in Las Vegas some time ago, and that we were doing business together.

The Patch said that he, and several of his friends thought that Mike was a "narc", a term used to describe an undercover police drug operative. I put on a surprised look and told him that this was total "bullshit", because I had been doing business with him for the past couple of year and had not experienced the heat (term used by the underworld for police intervention or arrests). The Patch said he knew I was OK, because "Tiny" was a friend of his, and had vouched for me. Tiny told him that he did a couple of deals with me, and everything was copasetic, but they were not sure of Mike. They started to call Mike a "Narc". I could see that Mike was now starting to get nervous, and about to lose it. I thought that Mike just might spill the beans, and say that I was the narc, and he was just an ordinary American visitor to Canada. After all, he had a distinctive American accent; therefore, he was unlikely to be a Canadian cop. I became concerned, and spoke up in Mike's defence, as a crowd of inquisitive people gathered around us like a bunch of hornets.

I looked at my watch, and stood up, and said to the crowd, that we were supposed to meet up with some people, and we were late. I said to Mike "Let's go, we are late for our meeting, we got a deal happening." Mike got up, and we said our goodbyes to our "friends," and we casually walked out, through the crowd. Then as we got out of their eyesight we moved quickly before this group (of ten individuals who were suspects in some murders in the Los Angeles, and San Francisco area) could grab us, and put their guns in our faces. God was my protector that eventual night.

A couple years later after my undercover work has come to an end, Eddie SENGER had a couple of young men to bring a shipment of cocaine from Florida to Vancouver. The cocaine was stored in a hollowed-out floor of a small boat that was shipped to Florida from Colombia. These young men picked up the boat in Florida and were being watched by the American DEA authorities, who followed them across the US to the Canadian/US border at Blaine, Washington. The RCMP drug section took over the surveillance and followed them to a location in the Lower Mainland.

Late one evening and under the cover of darkness, these young men then proceeded to tear the boat apart and remove the packages of cocaine for "Big Time EDDIE ", who was eagerly waiting to cash in on his shipment. The RCMP Drug Section members arrested these two men, and they went to jail for a short time. They eventually made the bail requirements and were released from custody.

It was a very short time later, that the body of " BIG - TIME EDDIE SENGER " was discovered wrapped in a carpet and dumped in the Delta dike area. So that ended the exciting life of Eddie SENGER. There is no honour among the criminals.

The Penthouse was a known place where the local Italian Mafia, and associated criminals hung out. After all, the Italian suspected crime family by the name of "VALLANTI" (name changed for reasons) owned the club. A couple of years after my operation ended, Victorio was found murdered in the living quarters of the club. It was common knowledge that the VALLANTIs ran a prostitution business in the club. I was approached on numerous times by the girls in the club. They asked me if I wanted them for a date, and if so, said I had to pay them so much for various sexual favours. I discouraged these girls for the time being and said that I had to take care of my business first. They seemed okay with that. I never returned to The Penthouse Night Club, after that very eventful night.

Mike and I concentrated on meeting Victor HANSEN, Mike's drug supplier. At first, Victor was not friendly towards me, and made it known that he almost got taken down while having several meetings with a young man, (whom he later found to have his horse parked out front - a term used locally by the drug underworld referring to the RCMP as horsemen, and our Musical Ride.

This young man was my predecessor, Harley DOIDGE, who was a pretty good narcotics undercover agent. He had that rugged facial look caused by adolescent acne. Unfortunately, Harley was not to enjoy a long life. I saw him, and his family at the Vancouver Airport, a few years later. We struck up a brief conversation and found out that they were going to Hawaii at the same time as my wife, Caroline and I were en route to Maui. Harley was having a difficult time breathing, could have been COPD, or perhaps because of his smoking habit, as I always saw him with a cigarette in his mouth. He died a few years ago.

Victor took his time even before discussing the subject of drugs. Mike and I had several meetings with Victor, and at times it seemed that we would not purchase any drugs from him. Then it happened. Victor agreed to sell a considerable amount of heroin to Mike, and Mike was to pay him directly. Victor agreed that I could be present during the sale transaction. Victor felt OK with Mike and was not aware of Mike's arrest stateside.

Several weeks passed, and then Mike and I contacted Victor again. We met at our usual meeting spot, Joe and Flo's Cafe. It had a name change a few years later. Victor was more relaxed, and Mike assured him that he, and I were business partners, and were doing a great business together. We would eventually be looking to purchase larger quantities of heroin.

Victor seemed OK, and eager with that. We set up a couple more meetings, and then Victor agreed to get some heroin for us. We arranged a meeting time, only this time Victor agreed to deliver the heroin, and he would be paid upon delivery. Everything was in order.

I drove to the pickup site and met Victor. He opened the passenger door of my car, and saw that Mike was not in the car. He looked very disappointed, and asked me where Mike was? I said that Mike had had to go to another important appointment and had told me to make the pick-up. Victor was now faced with a dilemma. He had the bundle of heroin in his hand, and he was not sure of me other than meeting me several times with Mike, and that I had been present during the last sale. He probably needed the money to pay for his commitments, and I was there with cash in my hands. Victor handed me the heroin, and I handed him the money, saying it was all there. His last words to me were, "Well if you are the man, then you finally got me". I said, "Vic, don't worry about it, I'll see you again. We will do a good business together."

I reached over and shook his hand. We said our goodbyes, and he closed the door to my car and walked over to his new Cadillac. I drove off in a hurry, and then I saw my cover members in their unmarked police cars screaming towards Victor at a high rate of speed. I was told later that four cars cornered Victor in his car. They came out of their cars with their revolvers drawn and were pointing them at Victor. He froze on the spot. He was arrested, and immediately had the big bowel movement. His first words to the arresting members were, " I guess I did not take my smarties today." Victor had just made the final payment on his Cadillac a few days prior to this drug deal. His Cadillac was seized as evidence and forfeited to the Government of Canada. It paid for some of my boozing.

Other members were assigned to search Victor's residence. One team kicked in his front door and surprised his wife. They searched throughout his house and found large caches of money under the mattress in the master bedroom, a result of his lucrative drug deals. This was seized. Victor pled not guilty for trafficking in heroin, and was represented by a lawyer, who was well known amongst the drug underworld, but did not have a great track record for getting his clients off. Victor was sentenced to twenty years in prison as he had a bad criminal record. Upon his conviction his house was later forfeited to the Government of Canada.

Years later, my second wife, Caroline and I were at the Vancouver Horse Race Track enjoying a few drinks between races. I looked over to the table next to us, and there was Victor with a woman, probably his wife, looking much older, and enjoying the afternoon as we were. He probably got paroled early in this great liberal left leaning society and was let out of prison before he served out his time. He did not recognize me. I did not go over to him, and say to him "Deja vu, did you wish you had not met ME in 1973? Guess what, I am coming for you again." I might have given him a heart attack.

There was another dramatic event in this drug raid. One of the teams that was assigned to kick in the back door of Victor's house; however, mistook the address, and kicked in the wrong door, (next door to Victor's house). To their surprise they found a pregnant woman nearing her due date, sitting in her living room relaxing. They quickly realized that they were in the wrong house. The corporal in charge, immediately sent his crew to the correct house, and being a real jokester stayed back with the pregnant woman, who was amused by him. He quickly called our repair crew to fix the door. The corporal kept in touch with this family periodically until the young child was born. I bet this child, and his/her family had a story to tell about their start in life. This corporal later went through the RCMP ranks and retired as a staff sergeant. He entertained the members with his jokes, etc., throughout his service, at several parties. He eventually retired and was part of a security services company. He unfortunately did not have a long enjoyable retirement. I attended his funeral a few years ago.

This was the last assignment I had as an undercover agent on the RCMP Drug Squad. It was a very exhilarating, exciting time with great memories.

Chapter 23

MY NEW HIDEOUT

I was transferred to Squamish, B.C. and continued working in General Duties in uniform. There, I spent about three years of a rather uneventful life. I got married and made some new friends. I had saved some serious money while working undercover, which enabled me to have enough money for the down payment, on a small (BC special house) on Kintyre Drive. I was also able to purchase a few household items. Various drug dealers that I had made drug purchases from, put a "CONTRACT HIT" on me, but they could not find me, and eventually gave up. I spent roughly the next three years going to court for the drug trials, and as a result was instrumental in putting a number of people in jail. I got paid a dollar per day "DANGER PAY TAX FREE," a small reward for putting your life on the line and enjoying the excitement.

As I was a senior constable, I got to train a young recruit for a short period. One evening while we were doing our patrols in the upper Squamish valley, we got a call from the Pemberton detachment to assist them in breaking up a fight between the Hell 's Angels motorcycle gang, and the local native Mount Currie

Indian tribe. We were quite a distance from Pemberton, so we were speeding along in the darkness on this narrow-paved road. A young constable Steve LYONS was driving the new police cruiser. We approached a left turning curve and came upon a small narrow bridge. Steve braked hard, and went into a skid, just before the bridge. I was not aware of Steve's driving skills, but I was soon to find out.

There was some gravel on the pavement, so as soon as we hit the gravel, we were basically on a bed of ball bearings, and were out of control. We slid into the ditch, and the new police car started to roll over to right side over some big rocks which were like boulders. Steve started screaming. I just put my right hand up against car roof to protect myself. The car made a complete one roll over to the right and was about to start on the second rollover when it hit a bunch of trees lining the riverbank. Then the car rolled back to the left and landed back on its wheels.

Steve received cuts on his face and arm, and he started to bleed, as he came into contact with the radio equipment, which was mounted in the front sear between the driver and passenger. Steve was screaming, it was pretty scary for him. We had a radio telephone in our police unit, which enabled us to communicate in remote areas. I heard two men talking to each other at the time, so I broke into their conversation, and told them this was a police emergency, and that they had to end their call. They immediately said their goodbyes and hung up.

I called our Squamish Detachment and told them that we'd rolled the car somewhere near a bridge in the upper Squamish valley road. I told them that we were OK; however, Steve had some minor injuries, and was in a minor state of shock. I had to get him out of the car as smoke started to come into the car. I also told them that I could see some sparks, and I could smell oil and gas, and that a fire could happen.

I hung up and got Steve out of the car in a hurry. We got up on to the road and saw where we were. God was with us that day, because had we rolled over the second time, we would have ended up in the raging Squamish River. Steve was a bit hysterical. I calmed him down and told him that we were lucky to be alive as we would have drowned in the river.

We waited for help to arrive which took about an hour. The smoke settled down, and the car did not burn up. The next day we looked at the damaged police cruiser, and found that the roll bar saved us, and minimized our injuries as the roof would have crushed in as we rolled over the huge boulders. The place where I held my hand against the roof was the only part that pretty much did not fold in. My body was pretty sore, but I thought nothing of it, just that I had to get back to work, and fill out the numerous reports. Our Detachment commander was not too happy, as we wrote off a new police cruiser with only 5000 miles on the odometer. Apparently, the next day a young kayaker drowned at that very same spot in the Squamish River. God was again my saviour that memorable day.

Chapter 24

DOMESTIC MURDER CASE

I assisted in my first murder investigation, which was headed up by Cpl. Garnet JACKETT, (now deceased at time of this writing) from the RCMP Vancouver General Investigation Section. A deceased female body had been found over a cliff on the highway between Lions Bay and Britannia Beach by two young men, who just happen to have made a brief highway stop to relieve themselves.

Prior to the discovery of the body, the Vancouver City Police received a report from a man named Jerry (not his real name), stating that his young wife, Elaine was missing. Because the body was discovered outside the Vancouver Police jurisdiction, the RCMP took over the investigation. Cpl. JACKETT put the pieces together, and the suspect in this case was none other than her husband. He was having a love affair with another woman, and wanted to marry her, but his wife was in the way. He had a young twenty-month old daughter, whom he brought to his girlfriend's house after he reported his wife missing and told her that he had to go work. His girlfriend was suspicious and called the Vancouver

City Police because he did not seem concerned that his wife was missing.

Cpl. JACKETT made some inquiries and found that Jerry had quizzed several murderers on how to commit a perfect murder. One of the murderer's told him that he would strangle his victim, put them in the bathtub, then cut their throat, and let them bleed into the tub drain. Then take away the body, and wrap it up in a carpet or tarp, and wash the tub clean. Then dispose of the body, which was pretty much what this suspect did.

Cpl. JACKETT arrested Jerry and after a lengthy interrogation was unable to get a confession from him. The other circumstantial pieces of evidence were unreliable and would not support a criminal charge. The victim's parents were so devastated, as they themselves believed that Jerry had murdered their daughter. They also wanted custody of their granddaughter, but Jerry insisted on having custody, and took his daughter to his parents' place in eastern Canada.

In the end he walked out a free man. His girlfriend had nothing to do with him, as she knew he killed his wife. Ironically, the little girl resembled her mother, so we often wondered what was in the future for her. Would her father abuse her? Would she question her father about what had happened to her mother? Would she meet with same fate as her mother, because she reminded Jerry of that murderous night when he murdered his wife?

Cpl JACKETT reviewed the file on a regular basis, amongst the other outstanding serious crime files, and I am not sure what happened in the end. Garnet and I talked about this case on the odd occasion. It was eventually passed on to other investigators to continue the investigation as Cold Case Files. Unfortunately, Sgt. JACKETT passed away in 2010, at the age of sixty seven.

In the end, I firmly believe Jerry murdered his wife.

On my many patrols, and investigations in Lions Bay I had chance meeting with some relatives of the well-known diamond mining De Beers family from South Africa. The male member (whose name which I cannot recall at the time of this writing) was in the glass business and was supplying windows to the many high-rise apartment/business offices being built in Vancouver. He was doing a very lucrative business and was at times overwhelmed with the sales. He wanted me to join his company and assured me that I would make more money than I was making in the RCMP. After much soul-searching I decided to ride it out for the low wages and interesting events in the RCMP.

Chapter 25

TRANSFERRED TO UNIVERSITY DETACHMENT

In 1977, a plain clothes position in charge of the General Investigation Section became available at our University Endowment Lands Detachment. I was offered this position because of my experience as an undercover drug operator and having an investigative background on complex criminal cases. Within a short time, I was scheduled to provide security for the visit of USA President Jimmy CARTER'S wife, Rosalyn, who was invited by the University of British Columbia to give a speech on mental illness.

At the time I was still living in Squamish about thirty-five miles from Vancouver. On that particular day, which was on a Sunday, I was speeding, or we like to call it "driving quickly", along the highway, in my unmarked police car, having gotten up on some heavy traffic between Squamish and West Vancouver. Well, you guessed it, I was stopped by a West Vancouver traffic member. He came to my driver's door, and I showed my badge and told him that I was late and scheduled for security in President CARTER'S wife visit to UBC. He said he did not care. I told him I was going to leave him there immediately, and he could call my Sgt at the UBC Detachment. I stepped on the gas and looked in my rear-view mirror. There he was completely beside himself. He eventually got his Chief, who was a former retired member of the RCMP to phone the UBC Detachment.

I radioed ahead to my Detachment and told them to expect a call from the West Vancouver Police Department. The sergeant in charge of the UBC detachment was not working that day but told me the next day that he received a call from the chief constable of West Vancouver. The matter was settled in the usual manner. Forget About It. It happens quite often in the big cities and police members speeding (sometimes without the siren or red lights flashing) in their unmarked police cars on surveillance and other investigations.

Well, I got to my detachment just with a few minutes to spare. I went to my scheduled area and waited for the arrival of Mrs. CARTER.

All of sudden Mrs. CARTER, appeared. She was walking behind at a bit of distance, following her staff and other important people. I stood to one side of this hallway and looked around for anything unusual. She looked in the direction of where I was standing, and she then stopped for about a second or so. I slightly smiled at her and she smiled back and then carried on walking. I was not sure if she thought she should shake my hand or say something which sometimes happens in these situations.

Mrs. CARTER'S speech was well received by the audience, and there were no security problems.

During my short time at the University Detachment, our office received a call from a man who was out fishing in the Georgia Strait, and while he was boating around, he found a partial human body with its head, arms and legs missing. He managed to tow it to shore where the BC Coroner's Service retrieved the body and transported the body to their examination room in Vancouver.

I immediately attended where the autopsy was to take place and met with the pathologist. He was an immigrant from the United Kingdom and spoke with a very distinct British accent. He also had that arrogant demeanour/attitude that he was the most important person on earth. I have in the past attended several autopsies with different pathologists and never experienced this sort of an attitude. They were friendly and explained what they were doing, and what I should take as exhibits to identity the deceased person and take whatever exhibits such as bullets, etc., that were important and part of my investigation.

The pathologist placed the body on his examination table. The body was that of a female as it had a blouse and bra strapped to her torso. This no doubt kept the remains of body intact, while the head, legs and arms were dismembered from her body during her trip along the Fraser River out to the Pacific Ocean. He carefully cut away at the blouse and bra and removed them.

While the pathologist was doing his dissecting, carving etc., which is what happens in autopsies, he made two slices in the very brittle parts of the flesh. I was watching him very closely. After he made the third slice, I could see the indented separation of the flesh. The pathologist stopped and said, "Did I do that?" I said "No, that is the stab wound." I was pretty sure this was the body of the young female that was murdered in the Chilliwack almost a year before. Her body was not recovered, but her three friends' bodies were recovered. She was shot and stabbed in the chest area and then thrown in the Fraser River. Her body got caught in the log jam in the river. The raging spring flooding of the river managed to flush out her body which floated out to the University Endowment lands, where it was discovered by the fisherman, in April 1978.

It was a bit ironic, because it was the same day that the accused in this case, Walter Murray MADSEN was about to be sentenced for this horrific murder. In my spiritual belief, it was God's way to end this case and justice was complete. The GULIKER family now had closure in this grief-stricken case.

This body was later identified that of Leola GULIKER. She was the victim in a multi murder case on July 18,1977 in Chilliwack which was reported in the Chilliwack Progress newspaper on April 5, 1978. It is available on internet with the full details of the court proceedings, etc.

Nothing of any great consequence happened during my tenure at the University Detachment. Included in this part of the transfer deal, was

(1) I was tentatively given a new unmarked vehicle to do my work, and

(2) I was given a small little wartime two bedroom house on the University Endowment Lands. I was on call twenty-four hours of the day for any major criminal matters. The rent for this house was only sixty dollars a month. A real bargain. It needed some work to make it more liveable to my standards, so I proceeded to strip eight to ten coats of paint off the wood trims around the doors and windows and refinish them to their original state. I painted all the walls. The hardwood floors were in a sad state. I decided against having to sand them, and re-varnish them at quite a cost. Carpets were popular back then, and it was cheaper, and warmer to lay down. So I purchased some bargain priced carpets on my own expense. I was not to enjoy all this for long, as police office politics played out, I found out that my career was now in jeopardy.

All in all, this got the sergeant in charge, and the two Corporals at the Detachment a bit jealous of my financial situation. They conspired together to get whatever dirt on me they could make my life a living hell. They decided to lay a complaint that I'd disobeyed a lawful command given by Corporal Rod ROUINDE (name changed) and supported by Sgt. Al CHINSON (name changed). They put together their colourful, untrue slander, (necessary paperwork for this charge), and forwarded to our Section NCO, S/ Sgt. Stan WICKION (name changed) at our Vancouver headquarters.

S/Sgt WICKION was briefly my boss at the Squamish detachment, before my transfer to the university detachment. He was now in his new position as a section NCO, so he decided to phone me late one evening after he got this complaint. He ranted, and raved at me, and made some threats. He sounded very drunk, and was known to have a drinking problem. I had no one that I could discuss this matter with. I was on my own. There was a saying amongst the RCMP members, that "you walk through the mine field alone, and if you don't step on a land mine, and don't blow yourself up, you will make it to other side OK".

The complaint was a result of a disagreement I had with Cpl ROUINDE. It referenced that I requested a particular suspect, who was involved in the numerous break-and-enter offences that were being committed in our area, as well as in Vancouver City. I requested that this suspect should be released from custody, and his charges negotiated as he was willing to help us, and the Vancouver City Police by taking us to his "fence". This is a term used by/for a person(s) that take in stolen goods, and pay the suspect little reward money for them, only to sell these stolen goods to some retailers, particularly jewellery stores, for larger sums of money. This suspect would work with our Joint Forces Unit composed of RCMP and Vancouver City Police members. This sort of arrangement goes on quite often with more informed, diligent police members; however, I was now dealing with police members with very, very limited knowledge of how to solve crime.

The S/Sgt in charge of this Joint Forces Unit at that time was a, RCMP member. He supported me in what I did and wanted this suspect to assist their unit in solving a lot of break/enter and thefts; however, he could not do anything to get me out of this situation.

Cpl. ROUINDE did my annual evaluation, and you guessed it. He down rated my performance to a borderline of getting me fired from/kicked out of the RCMP for failing to carry out his order. His lawful command was that I was not to interfere with the status of this theft suspect. This suspect was to be sent to jail, and his charges were to be processed.

Cpl. ROUINDE was not concerned with solving any of the outstanding offences and recovering any stolen goods. I was given my so-called "official warning" by Superintendent Dan HOMPANS (name changed)

It was several months later that I saw Supt. HOMPANS in his uniform walking/swaying down the hallway in our RCMP headquarters bouncing off the walls. He was avoiding eye contact with me. I stopped and looked at him in a very disgusted way. As I was not in uniform, I did not have to salute him. I could smell liquor on his breath as he passed by me. Perhaps he was having "a moment", before his imminent retirement, which did happen a short time later. You can be the judge in how I felt. Should I have confronted him on his bouncing off the walls on his drunken state, and tell him he was a disgrace to the RCMP? I believe "this UNFORTUNATE CHARACTER", got my message.

I could only conclude that this experience I had with these, four senior (what I can describe as four lunatic amigos) ranking members gave me an understanding of how this force was functioning. The general public deserved much better professional policing. ROUINDE, being a couple of years older than me, died a few years later of kidney failure. WICKINO, and HOMPANS also had shorter lives, and are now deceased because of health problems.

ME SOMETIME AFTER MY RETIREMENT

MAY 20, 2021, AWARD PRESENTATION – 43 YEARS AFTER MY
GUNFIGHT IN BURNABY.

Commanding Officer's Commendation

Corporal Merv Korolek
Regimental No. 27726

is officially commended for bravery for his involvement in a member involved shooting incident on April 22, 1979 at Burnaby, British Columbia.

Corporal Korolek and other members of Burnaby Detachment responded to assist with the stop of a vehicle with 7 occupants. While identifying and removing occupants from the vehicle, Corporal Korolek located live .303 caliber and .22 caliber bullets. Another member subsequently located a sawed off shotgun in the trunk. A passenger from the vehicle then pulled a sawed off shotgun from the back of his pants and shot a Constable who had been approaching him. Two police officers were injured by the shot, one quite seriously. Corporal Korolek drew his service revolver and shot at the shooter. The shooter grabbed the injured member's revolver and pointed it at police. Corporal Korolek tactically repositioned and controlled four other occupants of the vehicle while continuing to shoot at the shooter who was then pointing a revolver at the injured member's head. Corporal Korolek was preparing for a head shot when the shooter fell over and dropped the revolver.

Corporal Korolek's courage and composure during the engagement of an armed suspect in an active shooting incident assisted in bringing this situation to a successful conclusion. His actions and dedication to duty bring credit to himself and are in keeping with the highest traditions of the Royal Canadian Mounted Police.

Deputy Commissioner Jennifer Strachan
Commanding Officer "E" Division

February 26, 2021

MAY 20, 2021, COMMANDING OFFICER'S COMMENDATION

CPL. ED ROE AND MYSELF, AFTER ME RUNNING INTO THE SWANP,
YELLING AT A RAPE SUSPECT, " STOP OR I"LL SHOOT YOU"

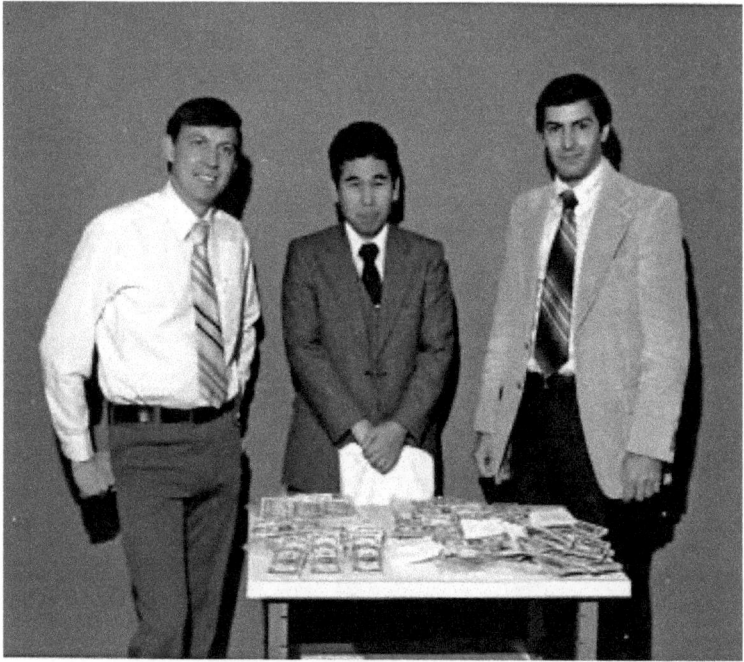

CST KAUTZMAN AND ME WITH THE VICTIM AND THE
RECOVERED MONEY.

GROUP PHOTO – APRIL 22, 2022 – WITH RETIRED S/S/M JOHN BUIS, RETIRED S/SGT JACK ROBINSON, OIC BURNABY DETACHMENT S/SUPT GRAHAM de la GORGENDIENE

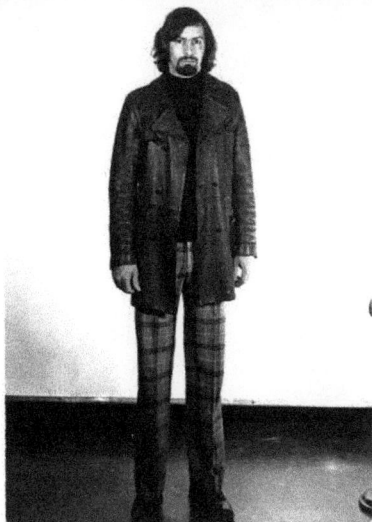

1973 - PHOTO OF ME AS AN UNDERCOVER DRUG AGENT

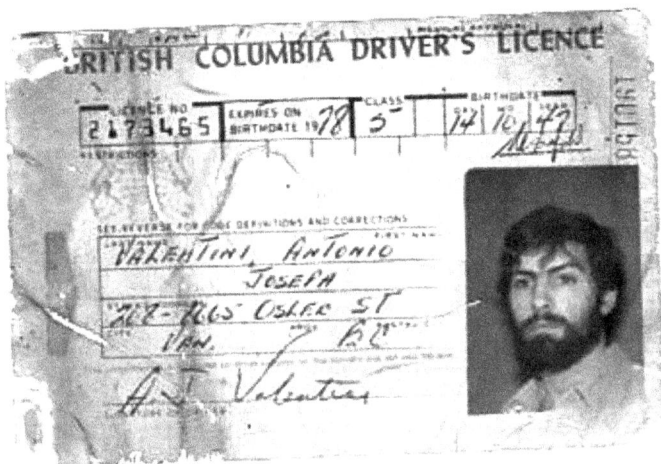

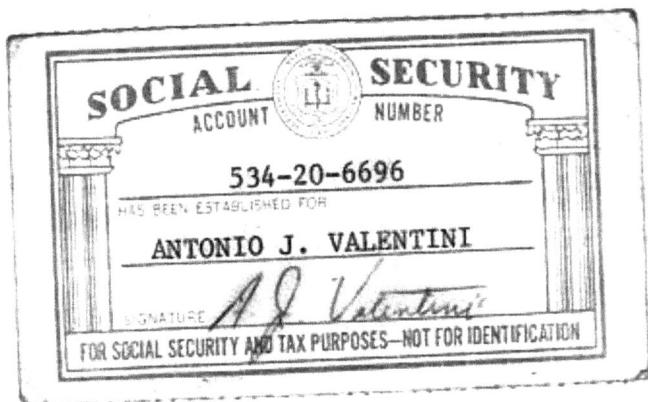

1973 – BC DRIVERS LICENCE IN MY UNDERCOVER NAME
- ANTONIO JOSEPH VALLENTINI

1972 – GIBSONS B.C. - FINDING A LARGE MARIHUANA
GROW OPERATION IN ROBERTS CREEK AREA CARED
FOR BY A LOCAL HIPPY GROUP

1970 - ME AS A YOUNG MOUNTIE

Chapter 26

TRANSFERRED TO BURNABY DETACHMENT

I was transferred to the Burnaby detachment where my first meeting was with S/Sgt. Fred PAHAL, who was the NCO i/c of administration. He was often referred to by other members as a father figure and was one of the nicest police members I have met and a complete opposite of what I had just been through. He said that I was most welcomed at the Burnaby detachment, as they needed a member with my experience. I told him that I did not believe him and related the circumstances of my transfer to Burnaby to him. He told me to put that all aside, as Burnaby was "Big City Policing" and said he, and the senior ranking members were looking for a member with my experience, and knowledge to train junior members.

Burnaby Detachment turned out to be one of my best postings of my career. Four months after my arrival, my career was in a real challenge, I was now in a real live gun battle, and fighting for my survival. The following chapter was submitted to the *Burnaby Now* newspaper after I read and disagreed with the contents of their story. I called the reporter, LAU, and he said he was not going to rewrite it, so I called his editor, and left a message. I did not get a call back, so I called the Burnaby Now newspaper again. I explained to the receptionist that I wanted to talk to the editor regarding the incorrect content of the facts surrounding the shooting incident back in 1979, because I was very much present at that event. She said that she will advise the editor, and they would get back to me. The next day, LAU, the cocky reporter called me back, and said he would now rewrite the story, and wanted me to email my version of the event to him which is as follows.

I did a lot of soul searching, and had some sleepless nights, on whether, or not I should include the following in this book. I have not mentioned or shared it with anyone except a friend, just a few days before the final publishing was being completed. They said I should include it in my story. I think that we all have PREMONITIONS, or forewarnings sometimes in our lives. Whether this was my PREMONITION or not, I think it made me more alert at the time. So here it is. **** Back in April, 1979, I had been going through a period of troubled times surrounding my recent transfer to Burnaby and I strongly disagreed with the way the RCMP handled my situation. The night before my involvement in a gunfight in Burnaby on April 22,1979, I had a restless night and had some crazy dreams. I had these crazy thoughts going on in my mind, that I would be involved in something the next day that was going to impact my life. Prior to going to assist constables BUIS and ROBINSON, another member in my patrol district suggested that he and I go for a coffee break. Once I heard BUIS and ROBINSON checking a suspect vehicle on Kingsway, I cancelled the coffee break and drove quickly to where they were. When I walked to the Lincoln and saw the characters there, I knew this was part of my crazy dream that I had had the previous night. When I found the gun belt with loaded .303 cal. ammunition in the floor well and .22 cal. ammunition on the back window ledge,

I made sure to position myself, so I had some protection once the shooting started.

I could not talk about this to anyone, because in the police community, I would be categorized as someone with some mental problems, etc. However, I survived.

Chapter 27

GUN BATTLE IN BURNABY
APRIL 22/1979

I recently read that the famous James BOND character actor, Daniel CRAIG occasionally Google's his name on the Internet, and he was amazed what was being said about him. I did the same, and found this article written by Alfie LAU from the Burnaby Now Newspaper, which caught my attention "I'm Tops in Canada – John Buis gets shot, I get an award!"

This article also appeared in the RCMP QUARTERLY, volume 76, No.1, Winter 2011. Some of the facts are not correct, so I (Merv KOROLEK, retired member of the RCMP) want to set the record straight. It is not my intent to glorify this event, but merely to correct the facts, and describe the human emotions, human action, and reaction that transpired in this tragedy. I want to congratulate Alfie LAU for his most deserved award on his journalistic qualities that he received from the Canadian Community Newspaper Awards Better Newspapers Competition (2010). However, in amidst of all the bad publicity over recent police shootings, I want to describe what happens to police officers when they are faced with the situation based on my own experience. Once the shooting starts, there is a lot of excitement, emotions kick in, and milli-second responses are made. Sometimes mistakes are made. When the shooting is over, some take the credit from others to overshadow their mistakes. Then blame is usually directed at someone, and some times criminal charges are laid. During my time in the RCMP we had to account for all bullets fired, and of course nobody wanted to admit that they missed their mark. Police officers in some of the other parts of the world do not have the same accountability. It is human nature to extend favouritism to people you know, especially if they work in your department. In the article this statement was written, "ROBINSON fired two more shots at GYULAY, hitting him in the right knee and left ankle." That is not correct, ROBINSON did NOT hit GYULAY with his shots. He missed, and I have outlined the actual facts of what went down prior to the shooting, and how it was impossible for ROBINSON to have shot GYULAY, because of where he was when he was shooting at GYULAY. I want to clearly state that I hold no animosity toward the other parties in this story.

I referred back to my notes that I made after this shooting, and the following is the true story. It took me back in time, and it was something that has been enshrined in my mind from the day it happened, April 22, 1979. Everyone, who has lived a short while has a story to tell, all are interesting stories, and some are more interesting and entertaining than others. However, I always believe that a crime story should be as accurate as it can be, but it depends on who is writing it, and what information he/she has at hand. As a member of the RCMP, I did my share of investigations, some in very complex cases. I also know about inaccurate information, and the problems that it can cause.

First of all, I want to commend both S/Sgt John BUIS and S/Sgt Jack ROBINSON (now retired) for their perseverance, and exemplary service in the RCMP. I am sure that coming back to the scene of the crime, especially for BUIS must have been a very emotional, and heart wrenching experience, knowing that things could have gone a lot worse for him, and Jack on the day they both got shot. I, on the other hand, visited that area often in the past, as some of my family business was in the vicinity of where I shot GUSTAVE JOHN STEVE GYULAY.

On Sunday evening April 22, 1979, at about 08:30 p.m., I (in RCMP uniform) went to assist BUIS and ROBINSON (two young plainclothes members of the Burnaby General Investigation Section) with their check of a suspicious vehicle, and its occupants on Kingsway and Imperial Ave., Burnaby. I parked my marked police cruiser behind BUIS and ROBINSON'S unmarked police car on Kingsway. BUIS and ROBINSON were having a conversation with the driver of the white Lincoln bearing Texas license plates. BARNES was standing with them near the rear of the Lincoln. I walked up to the driver's side of the Lincoln. From my police experience, I could see that the male occupants in the car appeared to be suspicious, and possibly criminals.

I proceeded to talk to the male passenger in the left rear passenger seat. I got him to step out of the Lincoln and told him to stand near the trunk. I asked him if he had some identification, and he provided me with his BC driver's license in the name of Kenneth Wayne SCHNELL. I then told the female passenger next to SCHNELL to get out of the car. She did not have any identification on her but gave me her name as Catherine Elaine GRAYSON (name changed due to privacy). I got her to stand near the front of the Lincoln. I then proceeded to ask the next female passenger in the rear seat to come out of the Lincoln. She got out, and also did not have any identification on her, but gave her name as Rose Anne DERRISH (name changed for privacy). Both girls said that they were from North Vancouver and were hitchhiking at the time they were picked up by these people and did not know any of them. I got Rose to stand next to Catherine near the front of the Lincoln.

BUIS and ROBINSON were still talking to the driver, whom I later found to be David Jeffery BARNES, aka Anthony Bergermin JONES. BUIS had gone back to his car to make some checks etc.

I searched the left rear passenger side of the Lincoln and found a black or dark green plastic bag on the floor. Inside it, I found a U.S. Army or Marine bullet pouch with a number of live rounds of .303 calibre bullets. I pulled it out, and put it on the roof of the Lincoln and said, "Whose are these?"

BARNES said, "It's mine."

I asked BARNES, "Were you in the U.S Army?"

He said, "No in the Marines."

I asked him, "When did you get a dishonourable discharge, or honourable discharge from the Marine's?"

He said, "In '73."

I asked, "Did you do some time in Viet-Nam?"

BARNES said, "No, they didn't send me there."

I asked, "How come?"

He said, "I don't know."

I asked, "Where is the gun to go with these bullets?"

I didn't get any answer. I said, "Open the trunk I want to check it." Cst. ROBINSON at the time was standing near the back of the Lincoln. He probably heard me, so he then told the driver to open the trunk. BARNES walked to the driver's side of the car, and pushed a button, and the trunk opened up. He then walked back and joined ROBINSON who was searching in the trunk. ROBINSON pulled out a sawed off .303 cal. rifle.

I looked further into the plastic bag and found a cleaning kit for a .22 cal. revolver, and I also saw a box of .22 cal. shells on the rear window ledge where SCHNELL was sitting. I asked BARNES, the ex-Marine, "Where's the .22?"

The ex-Marine said, "It's in the States." I did not believe him and thought it ought to be in the car somewhere.

I then proceeded to have a casual conversation with the two female hitchhikers. They seemed a bit scared. I am sure that they had wished that they had been somewhere else at that moment. Cst. BUIS was in his unmarked police car with the sawed off .303 rifle, and I assumed he was getting some more information.

Just then, another male occupant, (later identified as Michael Ralph BEAUREGARD, twenty-three years of age in 1979, from Beakon Falls, Connecticut) got out of the right rear passenger seat, and so did Gustave John Steve GYULAY (twenty-six years in 1979, from New Westminster, B.C.), who was sitting in the front passenger seat of the Lincoln. They were casually walking and talking quietly to each other on the grass/sidewalk area near the right side of the car. Then they walked to the front of the Lincoln but kept the front passenger door opened. They kept looking in my direction and saying something, which I could not hear. I got the impression they were concerned that I was asking too many questions, and that I had found the ammo belt, and cleaning kit. They probably wished that I had not found those items.

I then told the blonde female passenger, (later identified as Patricia Anne BENNETT, GYULAY'S common law wife, and the last person in the Lincoln) who was sitting in the middle of the front seat, to slide herself over to the driver's door, and come out of the car. She looked straight ahead, and seemed very worried about something. She was very tense. GYULAY then walked back to the open front passenger door. BENNETT had a brown paper bag in her right hand. I said to her, "Bring that brown paper bag with you." She turned to her right, probably to make contact with GYULAY, and then proceeded to slide herself towards the driver's side. I now believe that she may have wanted to discreetly pass the shotgun shells to GYULAY, but was a bit nervous, as I was looking right at her at the time.

At about the same time as BENNETT was sliding towards me, GYULAY leaned down near the front passenger seat, and grabbed something, which I could not see, and put it into his back pocket, or the back waistband of his pants.

I grabbed the brown paper bag, suspecting the .22 cal revolver was in it, and asked her, "What's in the brown bag?"

She replied, "Just some stuff, Cookies." (She was right. It contained cookies. I placed it on the hood of the car)

At the same time GYULAY stood up and kept the front passenger door open. He continued talking to BEAUREGARD. I could see that GYULAY now had a very stern, cold expression on his face when he was talking to BEAUREGARD, who also had a very cold, stern expression on his face. I knew something was going to happen, but I did not know when. I decided to remain calm, as I had been throughout this whole ordeal.

As BENNETT stepped out of the Lincoln, one loaded blue shotgun shell fell out of the front seat, and onto the ground. There were three live/loaded shotgun shells on the seat. I reached in, and picked them up in my right hand, and said to BENNETT and SCHNELL, who was standing to my right, "Where's the shotgun?" No one said anything. Everyone was tense.

I held up the shotgun shells in my right hand and said to Cst. ROBINSON, who was standing near the open trunk of the Lincoln, talking to BARNES, "There are shotgun shells here." ROBINSON, who was looking in my general direction, nodded his head, so I assumed he'd heard me and would note that there was a shotgun in this car somewhere, and would proceed to ask BARNES, where it was. At this time there were vehicles driving by, so it was possible that ROBINSON did not hear me over the traffic noise. Darkness had started to settle in.

BUIS walked over to the right side of the Lincoln and approached GYULAY. BEAUREGARD immediately started to walk towards the front of the Lincoln. I kept my focus on BEAUREGARD. Then I heard BUIS shouting, "No, no, no". I looked in his direction. He put up his hands in the air, and at the same time was walking backwards fast. I thought he was trying to get back to his police car for cover. I saw GYULAY pull out the double barrel sawed off shotgun from the back waistband of his pants with his right hand

and started to run towards BUIS. BUIS was approximately five feet from GYULAY, when he fired one shot at BUIS. It was a very loud bang. I could see a two foot (in diameter) yellow, blue flame come out of the shotgun barrel. The force of the shot lifted BUIS up in the air, and he came crashing down onto the ground. After the first shot went off, all the suspects/occupants immediately started to scream, and shout. I thought the shotgun blast hit BUIS in the stomach, and groin area. It looked pretty bad. I knew then what I suspected and hoped that it would not happen. I was now in a major "fight for your life" gun battle.

I was standing near the driver's door of the Lincoln at the time. I quickly took my revolver out, and fired a shot at GYULAY, hitting him in the right side of his chest. (GYULAY was later taken to the hospital where a bullet was removed from his liver. The RCMP CRIME LAB matched up this bullet as being the one fired from my service revolver. I still have that bullet and other bullet exhibits and shells from that day. They were given to me upon the termination of this case. I also have copies of photos surrounding the investigation, including one of the injuries sustained by BUIS on his terrifying day). It is amazing how alert one can be in the most intense situation. There I was, very alert. I could see the bullet leave the barrel of my revolver and make an indentation in GYULAY's jacket. We had slow velocity bullets back then. I said to him, "Hold it right there." It had no effect on him. He was charged up, and his adrenalin was flowing. As was mine. Did he show signs of a determined killer? You bet he did. Did I have the makings of a killer? You be the judge. It was probably no different than anyone else who was facing this situation.

At the same time, I could see in my peripheral vision, ROBINSON running back to his police car. He had not drawn his police revolver at this time. SCHNELL was ducking down against the left rear side of the Lincoln. BARNES was running at me on my right side. (I did not know until after everything settled down that BARNES and ROBINSON had been hit, and slightly wounded from the same shotgun blast that struck BUIS. They were in a direct line with the direction of gunfire from GYULAY's shotgun. GYULAY was using birdshot shells, which at close range make an awful mess, and can be fatal). On my left, I could also see the two innocent hitchhikers who were standing a fair distance in front of the Lincoln. They were screaming loudly. I could also see BEAUREGARD, with a very determined aggressive look on his face running in front of the Lincoln toward me. GYULAY then turned to his right, and looked at me, and pointed the shotgun in my direction. I suspected he probably had the other shotgun barrel loaded with a live round. (I had just taken the other live shotgun shells from the front seat of the Lincoln, limiting his upper hand in this gun battle). I did not want to lose my head that day, so I ducked behind the Lincoln, and put my revolver hand over the roof of the car and fired two quick shots at GYULAY. I was hoping that I might have hit him, or to draw his fire, and distract him so that ROBINSON could get back to his car and call for backup. GYULAY fired the shotgun, and nobody got shot with that round.

ROBINSON was now back behind the driver's door of his police car and was talking on the police radio. I assumed he was in contact with the detachment asking for assistance. (Later it was found that he was on the wrong channel, and I believe that the detachment dispatcher, Lori MERKEL did not hear his call, but she got a 10-33 call (OFFICER IN TROUBLE) from another member believed to be Cst. Bob McLEOD, who happened to be in the vicinity, and had seen what was happening). I could see BEAUREGARD coming at me with this killer look on his face, determined to cause me some problems. My demeanour changed, I was now a possible killer, and gone to the edge of the dark side. I pointed my revolver at BEAUREGARD's head, and said, " Put your _____ hands over your head and hit the _____ car." He under-stood my message immediately, and put his hands over his head, and started screaming. BARNES was now crouching down next to SCHNELL. They were also screaming loudly.

Darkness was setting in, so it was difficult shooting at GYULAY. I leaned over the roof of the Lincoln, and fired another quick shot at GYULAY, who was still standing up, looking at my direction. He seemed to buckle down after I shot at him. I believed I'd hit him in the leg area (later examination showed GYULAY was hit in the right knee. The bullet went through the knee area and was never recovered). I fired another quick shot at GYULAY who was moving about. I thought I hit him because he reacted immediately after my shots and fell to the ground. That bullet may have been the one later found lodged in his left foot (*1).

GYULAY was now crouching down, and dragging himself towards BUIS, who was a few feet away. I stepped closer to the rear of Lincoln and was about fifteen feet away from him. I heard and now saw ROBINSON shooting his revolver and was pointing it in GYULAY's direction. GYULAY was already crouching near BUIS possibly using him as a shield. (There is no way that ROBINSON's bullets could have struck GYULAY as ROBINSON claimed). I lined up my revolver with two hands and was going to shoot him in the head as shooting him in the chest area had no effect on him. I pressed the trigger, but it just clicked, and no bullet came out. It was a misfire, and it looked like I had defective ammunition. I fired it again, and it clicked again. I realized that I was out of ammo. I was pretty disappointed at everything in that millisecond, including the RCMP, for issuing us defective weapons, and ammunition. However, I was not going to give up, and I fully intended to finish the job.

GYULAY was searching for BUIS's service revolver. I ducked behind the Lincoln again. I shouted at all the screaming suspects, who kept turning around ,looking at me "All of you, put your _____ hands on top of your head and hit the _____ car." I must have looked like a pretty crazy deranged cop, but it had the right effect, and they obeyed me.

They yelled back at me. "Yes, OK, OK, don't shoot. Please don't get us shot." Just how polite they were for saying "please", that is debatable.

I pointed my revolver at BARNES and BEAUREGARD. I yelled at them, "Don't move." I had all the suspects/occupants lined up against the Lincoln, and the two screaming hitchhikers in front of the Lincoln.

I unloaded my revolver and loaded it up with live ammunition. BARNES said to me, "Don't get us shot up." I said, "Shut up. Don't move."

*** There was some information I believe that came from one of the hitchhikers. She said that they saw BENNETT take out the 22.cal pistol which she had in her waist band of her dress and point it at my left side about four feet away. The hitchhiker said that I grabbed the revolver and threw it under the Lincoln. I believe that I did not do it, as my hands were occupied. I suspect in all the commotion that one of the male suspects, possibly BEAUREGARD, grabbed the pistol, and threw it down. Or she may have thrown it down on the ground herself. I believe that this pistol was tested later and found it could have fired a live round. But, spiritually speaking, as some of our members jokingly called ourselves, "God's Messengers", God was at my side that day and I persevered. ***

I pushed BENNETT up against the front of the Lincoln and stood behind her. She had her hands over her head and was screaming. BUIS was lying on the ground face down, motionless. I thought the shotgun blast with that large fireball had hit him in the stomach, and lower part of his body, and it might have killed him, or he was very seriously injured. GYULAY had already thrown his shotgun on the grass to his left side, and now had BUIS's service revolver in his right hand. GYULAY pointed the service revolver down at BUIS. ROBINSON and GYULAY were having a heated conversation. I could hear GYULAY saying something like, "I will kill him."

I pointed my revolver at GYULAY and said, "Drop your gun."

He said, " No I am not. I got him I will kill him. Give me your guns. As a matter of fact, you come here." I thought he was crazy with that remark because I had other plans for him.

GYULAY was waving BUIS's revolver around in the air, and then pointed it in my direction, so I leaned back down behind the Lincoln for cover. I pointed my revolver at the suspects lined up against the Lincoln and told them, "Don't move." They all continued screaming. I knew I had this part of the situation contained, but I did not know if any help was coming. I was determined to finish GYULAY off for what he did to BUIS. I was pretty much in control, and steady throughout this whole ordeal.

I grabbed BENNETT around her neck with my left arm and brought her up against the front of me. She would be my cover. I had my revolver in my right hand, cocked, and ready to fire. I pointed it at her head and said that we were going for a walk. She was screaming. I started pushing and walking BENNETT towards GYULAY. I planned to get close enough to GYULAY to shoot him in the head. We walked a few steps towards GYULAY. Just then Cpl. Jim BELL drove his police cruiser over the curb on Russell Street at GYULAY, who leaned over backwards, and passed out.

My bullet, which was later removed from his liver, did finally have its effect, and he lived to serve out his arrest, and time in detention. The bullet in GYULAY's foot was not removed because it was not life threatening. Plainclothes members, Csts. John McKAY, Bob POWELL and uniform members, Csts. DEMERS and Bob McLEOD arrived, and made the arrests.

Prior to the arrival of the ambulance, Cpl. Jim BELL examined GYULAY for injuries, and found three bullet wounds on GYULAY's body. He asked both Cst. ROBINSON, and me as to where we both shot him. Cst. ROBINSON spoke up first and said that they were all his shots. Cpl. BELL asked me where I shot GYULAY, I remember telling him that I shot him, but someone else will determine that (*1).

The Burnaby Fire Department, kindly assisted the Burnaby RCMP. members by using their big fire trucks to block traffic from Imperial and Kingsway around the crime scene. The Vancouver City Police arrived in several cars and offered their assistance. BUIS, ROBINSON and GYULAY were taken away by ambulance.

I went back to the Detachment where various members came into the briefing room. We discussed what had happened surrounding this gun battle. I did not say much at the time. It was not a proper briefing, but more of a "get it off your chest discussion." I was glad to hear that BUIS and ROBINSON would be OK, but was not glad that GYULAY was alive.

Inspector TORRESAN, 2i/c of the Burnaby Detachment came to see me in the briefing room. He was concerned about how I was feeling. I told him I had spent a year (January to December 1973) of my R.C.M.P. career as an undercover agent/operator in the Vancouver Drug Section. I had dealt on a regular daily basis with hardened underworld characters, some of whom were killers/murderers in their own right, and had been shot/wounded, and were still carrying on in a life of crime. I had learnt to spin them BS stories to save my life, and I had survived to this day. (This is a whole other story for another time). He asked me why I didn't pull out my revolver sooner when I found the ammo belt, and I suspected something dangerous was about to happen. I told him that I was recently transferred to Burnaby Detachment on a disciplinary matter, which was more of a personality clash with the university detachment NCO's (*2) for doing something a lot less than this. I did not want to lose my job. I told him that I did not have much faith in the system. Insp. TORRESAN, was a little sympathetic, and told me to come in the next day to work, and to forget about taking some time off to settle the nerves, so to speak. I told the Inspector that I would be there the next day for my shift. I had a sleepless night with a few nightmares, which continued for several days, but that is life. I am sure BUIS and ROBINSON had their fair share of nightmares over this incident. I am sure it happens to everyone who has been through an ordeal such as this. I came to work and weathered the rumours of what was going to happen to me with the possibility that my career may come to an end.

I got a lot of gratitude from some of the members-mostly the uniformed side. A few kept their distance for whatever reason, and I was OK with that. Some made comments that if I had not been there, we would most likely be burying two of our members. I was more concerned about my career being terminated, as there were some rumours that they (RCMP) would charge me with attempted murder for what I said and did to the suspects/occupants of the Lincoln. But I was the product of working undercover in the drug underworld, as an agent/operator dealing face to face with hardened underworld figures, some of whom were killers on the loose. There was an odd occasion when I had to effectively threaten and inflict pain when they ripped me off on a drug deal. The assault or pain inflicted on them was just short of them not going to the hospital for treatment, but they got the message. Such was life on the street, in the drug underworld. A few days later, Cpl. Al CHATER now deceased several years ago since the writing of this publication who worked on another watch, came to me and said that he was thankful that it was me there that day because he was not sure that he, (and there may be others), could have pulled it off, and survived. I was thankful for his comments.

GYULAY was sentenced to life in prison.

Several R.C.M.P. members, and I had some concerns about our ineffective .38 cal. revolvers, so we purchased .357 Magnums, which resemble a .38 revolver, and is a more effective weapon. We carried them on duty, without the knowledge of some senior officers. The RCMP have better equipped weapons today.

When the dust finally settled, so to speak, on October 22, 1980, Asst. Commissioner H. (Hank) JENSEN, who was the Commanding Officer of District 1, "E" Division, was so kind as to write me a letter of commendation.

I quote, "On April 22, 1979, you provided cover for Constables BUIS and ROBINSON while they checked a suspicious vehicle carrying seven occupants in Burnaby, B.C. Shortly after your arrival at the scene, an occupant of that vehicle fired a sawed-off shotgun and seriously injured Constable BUIS.

You responded decisively and in return fire you wounded the assailant, Gustave John Steve GYULAY, who in the interim held Constable BUIS hostage and threatened to kill him if anyone made a wrong move. Your actions were instrumental in gaining control of this critical situation and successfully disarming GYULAY and preventing further injury or loss of life.

I commend you for your decisive action, courage and presence of mind, which you displayed under these most difficult and trying circumstances. Please accept my personal thanks for this admiral performance of your duty in the face of danger to yourself and others present at the time."

In normal circumstances, a member of the RCMP, who experienced similar frightening moments in his/her life, would have received a Letter of Commendation from the Commissioner of the RCMP. However, there were rumours that Asst. Commissioner JENSEN and the Deputy Commissioner in charge of all "E" Division (all of B.C.) at the time had some personality conflicts. JENSEN was not able to get specific documents, particular to this case forwarded through the Deputy Commissioner to our Headquarters in Ottawa and the Commissioner.

I was thankful to receive the letter, which was later framed in appreciation by BUIS, who also received a letter of commendation, as did ROBINSON for his efforts from A/Commissioner JENSEN. I had a lot of respect for A/Commissioner JENSEN, who was later transferred to our Ottawa HQ'S and was promoted to deputy commissioner. Sometime later while attending the police academy in Ottawa, I had a short visit with him, and told him that I really appreciated for what he had done for me.

Inspector John McKAY (now retired from the Vancouver City Police) was the young RCMP constable who came to make the arrests after GYULAY passed out. He was known by a friendly nickname, "MACHINEGUN MCKAY". He possessed several legal weapons and was a martial arts expert with a black belt in karate. He was and is very much a lethal weapon himself. I have known him to be a strong, no-nonsense guy. You would be best to have him on your side. He had a very interesting police career, first with the RCMP, then Winnipeg City Police Department, and finally with the Vancouver City Police Department. There is a true 'MACHINEGUN MCKAY' and that is his son, who is in the Canadian Army and is a machine-gunner having recently served in Afghanistan. I wish him a safe journey in his service with the Canadian Army. Inspector John McKAY (Rtd) continues to train people in martial arts today. Prior to his retirement from the Vancouver City Police, he sought out the status of GYULAY.

The following is his version of what happened on that dreadful day from where he was positioned, and his subsequent follow-up investigation into the possible bombing of the New Westminster Court Building, and jail breakout.

"On April 22, 1979, Bob Powell and I were working the afternoon shift in plainclothes. We were members of Burnaby GIS Fraud Section; however, we worked rotating shifts taking in major investigations apart from our normal duties.

We heard Merv KOROLEK, covering Csts BUIS and ROBINSON at Kingsway, and Imperial, and decided to head up as a cover unit. Just short of our arrival on scene the gun battle erupted, and as we pulled in from behind, I could see Gus Gyulay laying down behind John BUIS's body on the sidewalk. I could also see a crowd of people around the front of the vehicle they had stopped. As we got out of our car, Bob POWELL got out on the same side of the vehicle that GYULAY and John BUIS were on. GYULAY was shooting at Bob. I got out of the driver's side drew my handgun and ran up behind the marked car that Merv had driven, and I peeked around the corner of the bumper about fifteen feet from GYULAY. John was unconscious and laying across the sidewalk with his head towards the curb. GYULAY had pulled his service gun out and was pointing it at Bob Powell by reaching over John's body. He had also stacked John's ammunition on his side of John's body. I have no recollection of where Jack Robinson was or where Merv KOROLEK was.

As I got into position, I could hear Bob POWELL yelling at me McKAY get down get down "She's shooting at you!" I found out later that GYULAY's girlfriend had a converted starter pistol loaded with .22 cal ammunition, and was shooting at me, but I have no recollection of that event, just Bob Powell yelling at me to get down. What a great partner he was. Somehow, I knew that GYULAY had been wounded. When I peeked my head around the corner of the car John BUIS suddenly regained consciousness and began looking around. I was going to try a head shot on GYULAY, but he cocked John's gun, and put it up to his head, and told me to drop my gun or he'd kill John.

I responded that if he killed John, I'd kill him even if he surrendered. I also told him I knew he was wounded and wasn't going anywhere. GYULAY then threw John's gun back over his own shoulder, and Cpl Jim BELL and I ran up and handcuffed GYULAY. I then went over to John BUIS, and the first thing out of his mouth was "Hey McKAY are my balls still on?" I told him they were, and I knew he was in shock. I didn't want to make his condition any worse.

Around eight to ten Vancouver police officers arrived in droves and began to help us out by assisting in handcuffing and searching the rest of the group near the front of the stolen car. I remember them being really angry that two officers had been shot. Whatever we wanted they were prepared to help us with, and I was never so glad to see them, as I was that night. Later EHS arrived on scene.

I was covering the group at the front of the car, and I heard and saw one of the females later identified as Patricia Ann BENNETT moving something with her feet as she was bent over the hood of the car. Someone else took control of her, and I looked down and saw a small pistol below the bumper. It was the one she had tried to shoot me with, and she was trying to push it under the car.

I took GYULAY to the Burnaby Hospital, and then to Vancouver General where he had surgery. I never saw him again. In return for no charges laid against his girlfriend Patty BENNETT, he pled guilty to attempted murder of a policeman, and got life in prison.

It is my understanding that when he shot John BUIS and Jack ROBINSON he had recently been released from jail in Manitoba for the attempted shooting of the chief of police at Steinbach Manitoba. Evidently, he had been dating the chief's daughter, and when the chief told him to get lost, he attempted to shoot him with a revolver. On that occasion the chief's tie became lodged between the hammer and the round, and failed to fire, thus saving the chief's life. I think he served eight years on that charge before he was paroled.

Gustav John GYULAY was my age, and he died in 2008 from Hepatitis C, which he incurred from intravenous drug use I suspect in prison, and from his time on parole. His was a wasted life.

We never had a debriefing of the incident, so I was never aware of where Bob POWELL went after we pulled up. Nor do I know where Merv KOROLEK or Jack ROBINSON went after the initial engagement. It seems to me that except for John and Jack we all went back to work right away, and the incident was treated as being "part of the biz." We all just carried on.

Within a few weeks, there was intelligence that Schnell, Lose and Patty Bennet had hatched a plot to blow up the New Westminster Court house to get GYULAY out of jail. The intelligence was pretty solid, and my new partner Jack Gallop and I were assigned by S/Sgt. Paul STAREK our boss to put a stop to the plot. Jack and I tracked down the plotters, and the attempt to blow up the court never happened......but that is another story.....
maybe...someday. "

*1 - There is no doubt a dispute whether it was ROBINSON'S or my bullets that caused the wounds to GYULAY'S right knee and left foot. Sgt. Darrel SHIELDS, who was 2i/c of the Burnaby General Investigation Section at the time, and the lead investigator in this shooting, met with me a day or two later. He said that from recreating the crime scene, the bullet wounds found on GYULAY matched the angle of gunfire from me shooting GYULAY. Those were my bullet holes in GYULAY and not ROBINSON'S. However, ROBINSON said he fired his gun in the direction of GYULAY, and later found out that there were bullet wounds in GYULAY'S right knee and left foot. He said that they were his bullets. Sgt. SHIELDS did not think so. SHIELDS told me he had to make ROBINSON feel good under this stressful incident, and it would be good for his character/ego whatever you want to call it. I believe that Sgt. SHIELDS said he would put it in the report that it was ROBINSON'S bullets that hit GYULAY in the knee and foot.

LET THE READING AUDIENCE BE THE JUDGE

1. ROBINSON was wounded (not seriously), as was BARNES who was standing near ROBINSON by the first shotgun blast that struck BUIS. ROBINSON immediately ran back to his police car, got on the police radio and made the call for help. GYULAY was on the ground crouching near BUIS, when ROBINSON fired his revolver in GYULAY'S direction.

2. Anybody who is wounded; however, slightly may be hindered by reaction time, and steadiness of hand, and could be slightly inaccurate.

3. ROBINSON was firing at a much further distance than I was firing at GYULAY, and at a different angle. ROBINSON was using a police detective short barrel .38 cal revolver, which can be inaccurate in distance, while I was using my regular long barrel .38 cal revolver, and a bit more accurate.

4. Darkness was settling in, and GYULAY was moving around at the time.

5. From ROBINSON's direction of fire, if he shot GYULAY in the places he claims to have shot him, he would have most likely shot his partner BUIS, who was on the ground near GYULAY. I was perpendicular to GYULAY and BUIS.

6. The bullet in the right knee was never located.

7. The bullet remained in GYULAY's foot and was not taken out at that time as it was not life threatening. I believe that he took this bullet to his grave. The mystery of whose bullet it was that was lodged in GYULAY's foot will no doubt be disputed. YOU BE THE JUDGE.

8. There were two bullet holes in the GOODYEAR TIRE STORE sign near where this gun battle occurred, which were never examined. Those could be ROBINSON's or mine when I fired my revolver wildly over my head to distract GYULAY so that ROBINSON was able to get back to his police car.

9. I believe that Cst. ROBINSON was wearing glasses/corrective lens at the time of the shooting, which maybe, a factor in the accuracy of his shooting.

*2 – I was transferred from University Detachment to Burnaby Detachment for discussing a case regarding a Vancouver City Police and R.C.M.P. project with Regional Crown Counsel, against the wishes of the University Detachment NCO's. This was in reference to a known informant to have his charges stayed, which I purported, for the information that he could provide for further benefit of the Vancouver City Police, and surrounding area R.C.M.P. detachments in apprehending additional criminals at the time. Regional Crown Counsel wrote a letter to the R.C.M.P., management on my behalf that he supported me in discussing this case, and there was nothing wrong in what I had done, and the R.C.M.P. management were wrong in the mishandling of my transfer, giving me an official warning, and the annual evaluation that borderlined me for dismissal. The Detachment NCOs' and the subdivision superintendent ignored it and railroaded me to the Burnaby Detachment. I realized then that if you were not part of that inner group, you could get dealt a bad hand. I liked to get the job done, and I guess I made a few enemies along the way, who I believe were a bit jealous of my results.

YEARS LATER AND FAST FORWARD

On March 15, 2020, Cst. BUIS (NOW S/SGT MAJOR) appeared in the Vancouver Province Newspaper with a colour photo of himself (with a moustache, holding a Mountie hat in his lap). Headlines " A COP SHARES HIS PTSD STORY." BUIS phoned me a few days before this article was written and said that he was going through some stress in his life and wanted to know how I was doing. I told him I was fine, and this shooting had not affected me in the past and was not my health issue at present. He did say there would be another article written up about this shooting incident, but he DID NOT tell me all the details of this story which appeared in the Province Newspaper.

When I read the article, I saw that, again the story of the actual shooting was incorrect. Again, the reporter, Lori CULBERT wrote that ROBINSON FIRED ONE SHOT AT THE SUSPECT AND THEN RAN BACK TO THE CRUISER TO HIT THE RADIO EMERGENCY BUTTON. ROBINSON BLASTED TWO MORE SHOTS AT GYULAY, WHO WAS STRUCK IN THE KNEE AND ANKLE.

That is completely incorrect and inaccurate regarding what transpired. When GYULAY shot BUIS, ROBINSON immediately ran back to his police car. He DID NOT take his revolver out and DID NOT SHOOT at that time. He got back to his police car and hid behind the police car door and was talking on the police radio. He then fired his revolver when GYULAY was already crouching down next to

BUIS'S limp body. ROBINSON WOULD HAVE ACCIDENTALLY SHOT BUIS AT THIS TIME. ROBINSON'S BULLETS ENDED UP IN THE GOOD YEAR TIRE STORE.

I SHOT GYULAY IN THE KNEE AND ANKLE. When GYULAY ran out of bullets and was now wounded, he dragged himself to BUIS's limp body and removed BUIS's service revolver. IT WAS IMPOSSIBLE FOR ROBINSON TO HAVE SHOT GYULAY.

I phoned BUIS after I read this article and told him that the shooting part of the story was incorrect. He said he did not give out that information, which I DO NOT BELIEVE. He said that the reporter reads the file and writes whatever. BUIS SUGGESTED THAT I READ THE FILE, AND THAT C/SUPT. BURLEIGH WOULD BE HELPFUL, AND WOULD MAKE THE FILE AVAILABLE FOR ME TO READ IT.

BUIS said that this article was about PSTD and he wanted other cops who were going through some stress to get professional help. ASIDE from all that, I am sure there was some coaching on BUIS's part to say that ROBINSON fired the shots that hit GYULAY in the knee and ankle.

On August 5, 2020, I met with C/Supt. Deanne BURLEIGH, i/c of the Burnaby Detachment. She said that she made copies of the above mentioned, file (of whatever I am able to read as I am now no longer a member of the RCMP, but a civilian). I only found then that Sgt.SHIELDS, did NOT state in his final report that there were, a total of five, (5) slugs that were found in the Good Year Store. In other notes in the file, he did write down that two (2) of the slugs were removed in one part of the Goodyear Store which were mine when I shot at GYULAY, when I fired my revolver over the roof of the Lincoln. Those other (3) three slugs were found in another part of the Goodyear Store had to be from ROBINSON when he shot in GYULAY's and BUIS's direction. SHIELDS deliberately left that part out in his report, perhaps to make ROBINSON feel a bit better or whatever you want to call it.

The following is a copy of my letter to C/Supt. BURLEIGH

OIC BURNABY DETACHMENT

Dear Deanne,

I want to thank you very, very much for having made the effort for me to read the file on August 5/20 at the Burnaby Detachment, surrounding my involvement in the April 22/79 gunfight. Merely calling me back on May 7/20, showed me that you cared. For that I am eternally grateful. That would have never happened back in the RCMP during 70's or 80's.

I should have read the file, back when I was at the Burnaby Detachment; however, if I had requested to review it, and questioned the accuracy of the report writing, this would have set off alarm's bells with Sgt. D. SHIELDS, and others along the chain of commanders. My job opportunities, promotions, etc., would no doubt be jeopardized.

When I returned to the detachment after the gunfight, Insp. "Torchy" TORRESAN immediately met with me, and wanted to know what happened at the gunfight. I told him that when I arrived at the scene, I could see that trouble was most likely going to happen. I let Csts ROBINSON and BUIS do their part in handling their investigation into the suspicious vehicle from the US and its occupants. I did find the gun belt with live rounds of .303 bullets, cleaning kit for a .22 cal revolver, and a box of .22 shells on the back window ledge. I questioned the driver and had a brief conversation with him (later identified as BARNES) and advised him to open up the car trunk. Cst. ROBINSON, who was standing near the rear of the car with BARNES, then told him to open up the trunk. Cst. ROBINSON removed a sawed off .303 rifle and gave it to Cst. BUIS.

Torchy wanted to know why I did not draw my gun and put them under arrest. I told him of my recent transfer to BBY DET and the senior RCMP Management giving me an official warning for doing something not as serious as this. I could not trust the RCMP with my future. I wanted my job to which I was very devoted to.

In last part in the series of the reports that I read, it does state that 5 (five), slugs were removed from the Goodyear Tire Store. Two of those slugs were mine when I was shooting at GYULAY after he turned in my direction to shoot at me with his second shotgun blast. I ducked behind the Lincoln at the time, and just fired two quick rounds in his direction which I believe bounced off the roof of the Lincoln and into the tire store. This was all in hoping to hit GYULAY, and also distract him from shooting at ROBINSON. At the same time, I could see in my peripheral vision that ROBINSON was running back to his police car. He did NOT draw his revolver at that time which newspapers, etc., state in their news article, with two quick shots shooting GYULAY in the right knee and left ankle. GYULAY fired the second shot not hitting anyone. ROBINSON got back to his car and was hiding behind the police car door and was on the radio. A very short time later he fired his revolver in the direction at GYULAY and BUIS. Those are the other three (3) slugs in the Good Year Tire Store. THIS ACCOUNTS FOR ALL OF THE FIVE (5) SLUGS IN THE GOOD YEAR TIRE STORE.

The RCMP did not do a ballistics test on those five (5) slugs. (1) SHIELDS did not want to know if those three were ROBINSON's because of the inaction, embarrassment, whatever you want to call it. If those three (3) slugs were from ROBINSON's revolver, he would then have to state those facts in his report. (2) could be that he felt they were of less or no significance in this case.

When the shooting was over, ROBINSON and I walked over to where Cpl. Jim BELL examined GYULAY and found three bullet wounds on GYULAY's body. He asked both of us who shot where. ROBINSON immediately spoke up and said those were his shots, which was total BS, wishful thinking on his part, because of his inaction of not responding when there was all this evidence in front of them. I told BELL that they (meaning the investigators and firearm analysis) would determine where my bullets landed.

I know that when I was shooting at GYULAY, he responded or reacted when I shot at him. I am pretty certain that the wounds in his right knee and the bullet in his left ankle (came from ME).

I am a retired criminal analyst having spent my last days in the RCMP, DCIAS (which was the Divisional Criminal Information Analytical Section at the time). I had a background career as a drug undercover agent/operator, investigations of serious rape, murder cases, as well as being selected to be the first liaison member to CSIS in Vancouver during the AIR INDIA BOMBING INVESTIGATIONS. I know about CORRECTNESS and ACCURACY, which are important when releasing crime reports to the media, and our courts.

Someone, I suspect gave their version (having been embarrassed of BUIS'S & ROBINSON'S inaction in this gunfight to the news reporters to favour Cst. ROBINSON shooting GYULAY).

I will end this letter with a quote from my wife's dearly loved, departed uncle, George, saying in his BRITISH ACCENT (he lived in London), "IT DOES NOT MATTER HOW YOU FELL DOWN, IT IS HOW YOU PICK YOURSELF UP," He always ended it with his jolly laugh. If you met him, he would have you in stitches, laughing all the time.

Feel free to call me if you want.

That is history. I will comment on this in my book, which I am calling, NOBODY IMPORTANT Just A RENEGADE COP.

Yours Truly,
Merv KOROLEK

(SEE THE LAST CHAPTER RE: AWARD PRESENTATION))

Chapter 28

THE JAMES HOLDEN GANG
Safe Attack & Over $250,000 Stolen

In 1982, a young entrepreneurial thief, and his young gang of bandits were pretty active and successful in breaking into houses, stealing private property, and not getting arrested for their adventures. This time HOLDEN, and an accomplice (Tom) decided to break into a house that was occupied by a Japanese family. Luckily no one was at home at the time and would not come home until later in the day. To HOLDEN and Tom, it seemed pretty routine until they came upon a safe stored in the basement, and this elevated their suspicions as to what was in the safe. Lo and behold, to HOLDEN and Tom the safe was locked.

The following story was extracted from the interviews of HOLDEN, and his accomplices, particularly the one who hid the money. This was most valuable, as it enabled us to recover the money, and probably saved their lives.

Once HOLDEN and Tom agreed that they would take a chance of breaking into the safe, they started looking around for some tools. They managed to find a pry bar, and hammer, and went to work making a lot of noise, and eventually broke the door off its hinges. Inside they found a lot of cash. They were really pumped up and could not believe their fortune.

They put the cash in a garbage bag, and made a quick get away, and went to the residence of another of HOLDEN's accomplices (Jack). They were over the top with excitement. The cash consisted of Canadian, and American green backs, and Japanese Yen, along with other documents like bonds. They found about $ 80,000 in Canadian cash and gave up as they got tired counting it. They felt there was more than US$100,000, and Canadian and Japanese currency. They took several thousand Canadian dollars and put the rest of the money in a black plastic bag and gave it to their accomplice (Jack) whom they were visiting at the time.

Jack was the custodian of the money, so he quickly jogged off into Central Park which was a block, or so from his mother's townhouse. He hid the money around a tree stump deep in the greenery, then returned home.

HOLDEN, and Tom and Jack trotted off to find a taxi. They eventually found one and went to pick up a couple of young girlfriends. Off they went feeling high with all the cash in their pockets. They took several taxis, and just got the driver to drive them around. If the driver was of East Indian descent, he got no tip. If the taxi driver was of Caucasian descent they tipped him twenty dollars. Going out to a restaurant was also on the agenda, but as they were under legal age, they could not order any booze. Their choice of a restaurant was, you probably guessed it, the Golden Arches - McDonald's. They satisfied their appetites by gorging themselves on McDonald's burgers etc.

At one point they went to Sewell's Marina in Horseshoe Bay, West Vancouver, and tried to rent a motorboat. Because they were underage, and with no drivers licence they could only rent a rowboat. So, they rented a rowboat, and rowed themselves around the harbour, and at one point they almost got themselves into trouble when one of the BC Ferries was coming into dock. They continued the driving around in taxis and eating, McDonald's burgers until the end of the day.

The Japanese family came home and were completely horrified that their house was broken into, as they had left Japan for Canada, and a safe life. What a surprise!!!!!!

I got called in by S/Sgt Paul STAREK i/c of Burnaby General Investigation Section and was told that I had twenty-four hours to crack the case. I was to arrest those responsible for breaking into the safe and stealing the Japanese family's money. My partner at the time, Cst. Brian FURLOT, and I set off to view the crime scene. There we encountered a very distraught Japanese gentleman, and his family.

We had our Ident Section attend at the scene, and search for fingerprints. We got lucky as our Ident Section uncovered a palm print. At that time, our investigators took palm prints of juvenile suspects, and they were saved at our RCMP Vancouver HQ Ident Section. I took the suspected palm print to them for a search of a likely suspect. The female Ident Member decided to stay, and work overtime. She called me within a couple of hours, and informed me that she had found a match, and they had matched to none other than James HOLDEN.

In the meantime, our interview of the Japanese victim revealed a bit of a shady deal in how he had brought approximately a million dollars in various Japanese Yen, and US currency into Canada in the previous year. He had opened a small cigar/ magazine shop in downtown Vancouver, basically a front for dispersal of corrupt money. There was guilt written all over his concerned face. We advised him that we would pursue this matter of his stolen money as quickly as possible and keep him posted on the progress.

FURLOT and I set out in search of HOLDEN. We found him bunking out in his friend's (Jack) place. After some interrogation we arrested HOLDEN's accomplice, Tom. We worked through the night, as they both told us about breaking into the house, and cracking open the safe, and finding a lot of money which they gave to (Jack) to hide. Early the next morning, FURLOT, and I knocked on Jack's residence. His mother had gone to work, and we arrested him, and took him into custody.

I did not waste any time, and went right to the point, telling Jack that we knew he hid HOLDEN'S stolen money. I informed Jack that this money belonged to one of the suspected members of the YAKUSA GANG, similar to the Italian Mafia, or the Chinese Thong Gangs, all ruthless murderers. If I did not recover the money, and they were released back to their homes, I would inform the victims of what transpired in the recovery of their stolen money. The YAKUSA will send their people to break into their (HOLDEN etaAl) residences while they were sleeping, and abduct them. They would likely torture them. One way or the other, even if the HOLDEN GANG did not tell them where the money was, they would end up floating down the river, and we would likely find them dead one way, or the other the next day. Jack immediately said he would take me to the money.

FURLOT and I drove Jack to Central Park, and we walked through the greenery. I was amazed that Jack found the spot where he had hidden the money. FURLOT seized the garbage bag full of cash, and we returned to Jack's house to retrieve the rest of the cash. While we were there, Jack's home phone rang. FURLOT answered and pretended to be Jack. The caller was the brother of HOLDEN's safe attacker accomplice, Tom but he was unaware that his brother was already in custody. FURLOT told him to come over. We waited about half an hour, and the greedy caller arrived. He was surprised that the police were there waiting for him. We arrested him and drove Jack and Tom's brother back to the detachment.

Further interrogation revealed that HOLDEN's safe attacker accomplice, Tom had called his brother late the previous evening to tell him about the bootie. Tom's brother was a small-time drug dealer and had an ambitious mind. He envisioned buying a house, and carrying on with his drug trafficking, but on a much larger scale. His dreams were dashed as soon as he entered Jack's house, and FURLOT snapped the cuffs on him. You should have seen his face as the click, click of the cuffs were fastened around his wrists.

All in all, we solved the crime, and retrieved most of the money, and other financial documents less a couple thousand dollars within the twenty-four hours I was allotted. Cst. Al KAUTSMAN assisted FURLOT with counting of the money. The Japanese victim was overjoyed that we'd recovered the money. We recorded the amounts of each currency, and then invited the victim to pick it up. Cst. KAUTSMAN and I had placed all the money on a table, and had the victim stand behind the table with us on either side and had our Ident Section photograph the return of the money to the victim. The victim had a very solemn look on his face. After that the victim's wife sat down and gave us the most impressive demonstration in counting the money. She was very fast, and amazing, and polite as politeness is very prevalent in the Japanese culture.

HOLDEN "etal" got the usual sentence of next to nothing in the juvenile court system. We were glad we were able to solve this crime, and retrieve most of the money, and return it to its owner, regardless of the questionable circumstances. Canadian Revenue Agency was notified of the circumstances surrounding this Japanese citizen's dealings, and the amount of money he had brought into Canada.

Chapter 29

HOUSE PARTY RIOT IN BURNABY

After being taken off plain clothes duty for interrogating, and applying some persuasive techniques to a murderer accomplice, I, and six other General Investigation Section (GIS) members were transferred to General Duties. I was working an afternoon shift in a supervisory position on one of Burnaby Detachment watches when a call came in that a house party had gotten out of control, and it appeared that the party goers started to destroy the household's property. I informed the detachment watch commander at the time, S/Sgt. Andy ANDERSON to get out the Riot Gear as we may need them sooner than later. He immediately mobilized all available members from other watches and got them to come to the scene.

I got there quickly as I could and found the situation a bit frightening. There were rowdy young, aggressive males, and females alike, yelling, and screaming, and drinking beer. Some of them started throwing things out of the house.

I did not enter the house but remained out on the street. I radioed the detachment commander and advised him of the situation. The riot troop arrived within a short time and assembled in front of the residence. I took the loudhailer and advised the crowd of rowdy people to leave peacefully otherwise we would arrest them. There were some decent people who decided to leave peacefully, and then there were the other troublemakers. I sent in the riot troop to remove the rowdy crowd.

One corporal from one of the other watches arrived with the paddy wagon. The riot guys started to bring the drunken fools to the paddy wagon. We just threw them in and stacked them up. Young aggressive men as well as aggressive young women were thrown in. Then came a more drunken male, who was absolutely feeling no pain, and was as jovial as could be. The paddy wagon was pretty stacked up, so we just threw him over the top of the others.

I told the driver of the paddy wagon to give them a nice memorable ride back to the detachment. He did just that. The last guy that we threw in, could not keep his beer in his belly, and decided to vomit all over everyone who was in his projectile distance.

The subjects were booked in for being drunk in a public place, and then placed in the holding cells. I went to examine the wrecked house. What a mess. They had smashed a big TV. There were beer bottles, and trash all over the house. There were holes in the drywall. I met with the young man whose parents were out at the time, and he had a very puzzled look on his face. He was very concerned about how he was going to explain this to his parents. I told him that he could call the detachment for further details and left him with the mess.

I finished the shift and went home. I came back the next evening and I went about my usual duties. Later in the evening, I had a meeting with S/Sgt. ANDERSON, who told me that he had just had a visit with the father of one of the young females that had been vomited on during the ride to the detachment from the house party. The father was most upset and wanted to press charges against the police. S/Sgt. ANDERSON was one of those no-nonsense guys and called it like it was. He told the father in no uncertain language that his daughter was given every opportunity to leave the party peacefully, prior to being arrested. She chose to be defiant and was arrested with the rest of the group. The fact that she got vomited on was her problem, and he was in no way sympathetic of her situation. He told the father to get out of his office and leave the detachment. He was not going to entertain his nonsense of pressing charges when the police had a difficult job to do, to maintain law and order, and protect property. That was the end of the problem.

Shortly thereafter, S/Sgt. ANDERSON retired from the RCMP, and accepted a job as a police chief for the Oak Bay Police Dept. on Vancouver Island. The RCMP lost a very good commander, one of the best that I'd worked with.

Chapter 30

MURDER OF A YOUNG WOMAN BY A JEALOUS BOYFRIEND

After several members of the Burnaby General Investigation Section tried to get a confession from a murder suspect, and with time running out, S/Sgt Paul STAREK, who was in charge of the Burnaby General Investigation Section decided to have Sgt Steve and me interrogate the suspect.

Steve was considered to be one of the best interrogators in the detachment based on his aggressive behaviour, and he went about bragging that he was the one solving most of the major crimes. A lot of the members did not believe this to be the case and felt that his skill was overrated. STAREK also knew of my capabilities as an investigator and wanted me to team up with Steve.

Steve and I quickly reviewed the circumstances of this case, and Steve said he would talk to the murderer first. Steve interrogated him for about an hour and half, while I made the notes of the conversation for him. The murderer did not admit his guilt. Steve decided that we should take a brief break, and we left the murderer alone, locked in the interview room.

After the break, I told Steve that I would take my turn, and interrogate him. Steve, being not so happy that he had not been able to turn this guy around, had no choice, but to let me take over the interrogation. Steve did not make any notes of the conversation that I had with the murderer, as I had for him. I took this as a deliberate act of him wanting me to fail, and not have any back up notes in the event I got him to confess. I proceeded to talk to the murderer for about half an hour. Surprisingly, I got the murderer to confess.

The murderer said that he was jealous of his girlfriend, and he was high on drugs. It was a case where a murderer has this infatuation of, "if I can't have her, then nobody can have her." They usually kill the person. The story was that they'd had a disagreement. She'd run away from his car and run towards a house that had a light shining above the front door. She'd knocked on the door, and a young man, who just came home from a drunken party with friends, opened the door. To his surprise, he saw the murderer stab his girlfriend in the back with a big butcher knife. She then collapsed into his arms. The murderer grabbed his knife and ran off into the darkness. The young man sobered up quickly and called the RCMP. Now he could NOT enjoy that needed sleep after a drunken party. The RCMP members arrived and arranged for the removal of the body. This young man was taken to the detachment where he gave his side of the story on what happened. He'd probably had a few nightmares since, and stories to tell his friends.

Late in the night I convinced the murderer to take Steve, and me to the murder weapon which he'd tossed into the bush. We walked through the wooded area, and amazingly the murderer pointed to where he threw the knife. We now had the big butcher knife, a crucial piece of evidence in this case.

The following morning Steve immediately met with S/Sgt STAREK in his office and advised him that he'd obtained the confession. SUCH IS RCMP BACK-STABBING. The rest of the GIS members quickly came to me in the morning and asked what had transpired in the investigation. I related the conversation I'd had with the murderer, and that I'd convinced him to take us to where he had thrown the soon-to-be recovered murder weapon. They all said that "big bully Steve" had falsified the information, and they knew it was me who'd solved this murder.

Chapter 31

ARREST OF RAPE SUSPECT

I assisted Cpl Ed ROE in the arrest of a rape suspect in the Burnaby swamp/bog land. We went to the suspect's house and knocked on the door. Cpl ROE could see that the suspect had left the house through the side door and run towards the bog area. I chased the suspect in this swampy area, I yelled at him, "Stop or I'll shoot you." Cpl Ed ROE yelled at him, "He means it."

The suspect stopped in his tracks. Cpl ROE ran up to the suspect, and handcuffed him, while I dug myself out of the mud. Cpl ROE told the suspect that I'd shot a man, who shot two of our members a few months back. The suspect uttered some words to the effect of. "Thanks and I am lucky I stopped running, or I would be dead." Cpl ROE laughed, and quickly got our Ident member to photograph the two us. There I was in my grey checkered suit with mud up to my knees with smiles on our faces, but "We got our man," who eventually went to jail for some time.

Chapter 32

RAPE OF A LABORATORY TECHNICIAN EMPLOYEE

Back in 1981, the Burnaby detachment received a call from Marjorie, a Lab Tech, saying that she had just been raped by a young employee from the janitorial service that was cleaning their office right at the present time. Marjorie's name has been changed to protect her privacy in this very frightening, horrific experience. Our general duty members arrived at the lab which was approximately two-or-three minute drive from the Burnaby Detachment, and arrested the janitorial employee, later identified as RANDOLPH BRIAN HARDEN.

Marjorie was picked up at a gas station phone booth not far from where she worked and was brought to the detachment as well. I interviewed Marjorie and she gave me a very detailed statement surrounding her very traumatic, horrific experience of being violated. I have never, during my time of being in charge of the Burnaby Morality Detail, or during my service in the RCMP, interviewed someone in a rape case that just happened within such a short time frame.

Marjorie stated that she stayed on working overtime cleaning up some instruments after other staff members went home upon the completion of their shift. She felt safe at the time as she had done this in the past, and it was OK, as the janitor and his assistant, HARDEN had been doing the cleaning duties at their lab for some time. She had work that needed to get done, so she'd chosen to work overtime, which was a very bad decision on her part.

Marjorie stated that HARDEN came around to where she was cleaning the instruments in the sink and asked her about them. So, she explained what they were etc. Then he left and went about his cleaning duties. He then returned a short while later and asked her more questions, so she answered his questions, and thought nothing of it. HARDEN then left.

HARDEN returned a short time later and came up behind Marjorie, and put his hand over her mouth, and told her not to say anything. She was quite surprised and did not know what was happening. HARDEN had a knife in his hand and put it against her throat. He told her he would cut her if she spoke up loudly. She could feel the blade against her neck. HARDEN then shoved some paper towel into her mouth. HARDEN then shoved Marjorie up the stairs to the women's cloak room and closed the door. Marjorie was frantic at this point and could not believe what was happening to her.

HARDEN then shoved Marjorie into a shower stall and told her to take off her clothes. She unbuttoned her dress uniform part way. He kept that knife against her throat, and she mumbled, telling him to remove the knife. He kept telling her he would cut her if she made any noise. Marjorie kept telling him in her frightened, mumbling voice to put the knife down, to which he said he would not do it. Eventually he took the paper towel out of Marjorie's mouth and told her to kiss him. Then he made some a comment that it was nice, and she replied that it was not nice. HARDEN kept threatening her that he would cut her if she screamed. Marjorie was shaking and was very frightened and thought someone would find her dead in the morning when they came into work.

HARDEN eventually put the knife down. What came next was a very frightening experience that Marjorie went through, which no human being should ever experience. I am not going relate the graphic details/motions of what happened to Marjorie, but eventually HARDEN was satisfied, and apologized to Marjorie. He told her that he would not blame her if she called the cops on him.

HARDEN then pulled up his pants and left the cloakroom. Marjorie put on her clothes, grabbed her purse and ran out of the building. She got into her car and drove to a gas station phone booth and called her husband. She told him that she had just been raped by the janitorial employee, named Brian. He told her to call the police.

I then brought HARDEN into the interview room and gave him the usual official warning. He said he would not say anything to me and that he wanted a lawyer. I put him back in the cells.

A thought going through my mind at the time, after Marjorie related her horrific ordeal to me, was how am I able to get this sadistic monster out of here gagged and in handcuffs. Then drive him to a wooded area that is frequently visited by coyotes, wolves, and bears. Take him out of the car, secure his feet, so that he cannot run away, remove the tape from his mouth, then kick him several times in the balls to which he would be screaming and alterting the wild animals. Then take out my .357 cal. magnum and shoot him in the groin area. I would watch him suffer for a while, then leave. The sound of the screaming and gunshot, and the smell of blood would bring the wild scavengers quickly to finish the job of getting rid of this monster. Justice would finally be done, and he would no longer carry out his horrible, horrific desires.

Marjorie's husband came to the detachment, and I spoke with him. He said he wanted about five minutes to talk to the rapist. I said that as much as I would like to do that, I could not do that, as we would both be going to jail for a long time, and the rapist would be dead in hell.

Marjorie was having a difficult time in dealing with her sexual attack. I told her that if she wanted to talk to me on anything at any time, she could call me. I told her that I was living alone at the time, and that she would not disturb anyone. One evening after midnight Marjorie called me at my home, saying that her husband found it difficult to be at home, so he took off on a hiking trip by himself. She was worried, but said he was an experienced hiker. We talked about various things in her life, and I was her sounding board so to speak. She eventually calmed down and apologized for phoning me so late in the evening. I told her, she could call me anytime of the day or night, and that I would be there for her. We ended the call.

I searched HARDEN's past criminal record and found out he had previous convictions for two other rape and sexual assaults. I put together the details of this case in a court brief and met with the crown counsel's office. I advised the crown counsel, Wendy YOUNG regarding the seriousness of this sexual attack, and that it had similarities to Clifford OLSEN, who was well known as Canada's horrific sexual predator/murderer. We needed to put HARDEN in jail forever, which in the Canadian judicial system does not seem to happen.

YOUNG advised me that she would pursue a Canadian Criminal Code offence for which the accused criminal having committed several similar offences in their past life, could be sentenced to an indefinite time in prison. Their case would be reviewed every three years. As criminals rarely exhibit good behaviour while in prison, and with the guards usually giving them a bad time, they continue staying in prison for another three-year term. However, for this to happen, we would have to bring the previous victims to testify in court. This would be a big undertaking as victims in these types of cases do not want to relive the past, or they have moved from where the offences took place. YOUNG bought on another lawyer, Susan ANTIFAEV to assist her in this case.

I proceeded to make contact with the previous victims. I found one of the victims, who was now living under a different name residing in Calgary. I told her the reason for our, (the police and our crown counsel) of contacting her, was our desire to put her attacker in her case, and who was now involved in another rape case, in prison for an indefinite time, as I could see similarities to the CLIFFORD OLSEN case. He was a dangerous sexual preda-tor. This would assist us in convincing the judge to sentence him for a long period of time in prison. The Calgary witness was most cooperative and said that she would attend court in Burnaby.

The other victim had moved from the Okanagan area from where her horrific ordeal took place. I spoke with her father, who was a former Nazi POW, who served out his wartime sentence in the area. He said his daughter was now working for Lufthansa Airlines. He was not very cooperative it could be because of his Nazi background. He said that his daughter would be coming to Canada, and he would talk to her about it. I spoke to him some-time later, and he said his daughter had gone back to Germany and would not assist us in this matter.

I had a further discussion with the crown counsel, and it was decided that we would proceed with the evidence from police investigators who were involved in these cases. It was a blessing that a very detailed statement from one of the Okanagan sexual assaults was taken by the Corporal (now an inspector) at the time, and was introduced as evidence, which was accepted by the court. The inspector also testified in this case.

The day before the court hearing, I picked up the Calgary witness from the Vancouver airport and got her settled into a hotel room. It was wintertime in Canada, and she was wearing a fur coat, which was quite fashionable in Canada at the time. I took a detailed statement from her as requested by our crown counsel. I rushed it to get it typed up and handed it to our crown counsel, Wendy YOUNG.

The next day I picked up our Calgary witness and brought her to the courthouse. She was smartly dressed in business attire and made an incredible impression in the witness box. She gave her evidence and was not shaken for being thoroughly questioned by the defence counsel. I then drove her back to her hotel, where she spent the night.

The next day I picked her up and drove her to the airport for her flight back to Calgary. We were standing at the escalator to where she was going to take it up to the departure level. I told her that she was a brave, courageous witness, and her evidence at the trial would most definitely put that nail in HARDEN's coffin so to speak. I wished her the best of luck and said I hoped that she would be able to find peace in her life and put this behind her as she moved forward. We shook hands. She stepped onto the escalator, turned around, and faced me as she went up. She had a smile on her face, then blew me a kiss. I blew a kiss back at her, and waved goodbye. It was like an ending to a Hollywood movie. There she was in her fur coat, with a smile on her face, having given evidence in a serious rape case, sealing HARDEN'S lengthy time in prison, also knowing that we may never see each other or make contact again.

In the end HARDEN was sentenced to an indefinite time in prison. I left instructions for the prison authorities to notify me should HARDEN be released on parole, so that I may notify the victims in this case. So far during my remaining time in the RCMP, I was not notified, so I assumed that either HARDEN remained in prison, or he died in prison, which I hoped did happen.

Wendy YOUNG would eventually be appointed as a Justice to the BC SUPREME COURT.

Chapter 33

RAPE OF AN OLDER WOMAN

Approximately one year later, I investigated a brutal rape of a fifty-two year-old woman, who looked a bit older than her age. It started out with the woman going out early one morning for a cup of coffee and returning to her apartment block in North Burnaby. When she drove into the underground parking lot, she noticed a man walking around in his bath robe. She had parked her car and started walking up the staircase to her apartment when she was accosted by this man, who slugged her several times in the face and head. She was bleeding and traumatized by the blows she received to her head. He then grabbed her by her hair and pulled her back. She dropped her purse, and some items fell out. He told her to grab those articles and put them back in her purse, all while he was restraining her by her hair. He told her not to shout or he would kill her. She was very frightened.

He then dragged her down the stairs to the parking lot and then dragged her to a place between some cars. He then removed her clothes. He threw her jacket over her face, so she could not see him. She was in a semi unconscious state of mind and was in a frail state with no energy to fight this man. He made some comment that he had been watching her for five days, and how she would feel being f****d by a twenty-three-year-old, which was his real age. He continued with French kissing her, with which she did not cooperate. I am not going to describe his sexual act, but it was a horrific experience for the victim.

This man finished his brutal attack and left her there amongst the vehicles. He disappeared. She went up to her apartment and called the Burnaby Detachment, who responded quickly. She was brought to the Burnaby detachment and an investigation continued to identify all likely suspects in the area.

One suspect was DAVID ALLAN BROWN, who was a likely suspect in a murder case in the area, whereby a sex worker had been beheaded, with only the skin in the back part of her neck attached to her body. It was a grisly scene. However, our surveillance unit followed him around during his noted scheduled hours and had not set up on him that particular morning, as he did not move around until sometime later in the day. It was the most unfortunate bad timing.

BROWN was arrested and put in the Burnaby detachment cells. I interviewed the victim in this case, and she gave me the details of what she encountered, and the description of the suspect wearing his bathrobe. I had a couple of members who were working on my Morality Detail to put a photo lineup together that was shown to the victim. She could not identify BROWN from the photos. When the photo of BROWN was pointed out to her as a possible suspect, she said that he looked a bit older than his photo.

A physical lineup was then set up at the detachment which was viewed by the victim. She had no trouble identifying BROWN as her assailant. One of our members attended at BROWN's apartment and met with BROWN's girlfriend. She said that she did notice that he had not been in their apartment that morning, and that he'd returned shortly before being arrested that morning. She did hand over his bathrobe that he usually wore. It did match the description of the one that the victim had observed on the suspect when she drove into the underground parking lot that morning.

The usual forensic evidence was taken in this case and stored away as exhibits. Unfortunately, DNA science was not accepted in the B.C. judicial court system until 1999, four years after I retired.

BROWN was eventually charged in this case. He appeared before a judge, and was ordered to remain in custody, until a court date was set up for his trial.

BROWN had a good lawyer, (who eventually became a judge), who, upon questioning the victim in this case, asked the victim if she wore glasses or corrective lens. She said that she did wear them. When asked if she wore them when she viewed the photo lineup and the physical lineup, she said that she did not wear them, as the suspect had beaten her so badly in the face and nose area that she could not put them on; however, she was able to see things quite clearly.

That was the end of the case. The defence lawyer said that was not acceptable, and the judge ruled in his favour as reasonable doubt. The trial was over then and there. BROWN was free to go. His girlfriend and friends, who were present in the courtroom during his trial, stood up, and cheered loudly. They were subsequently scolded by the judge and told to leave the courtroom.

BROWN's lawyer looked at me, with a "look" that said he was just as surprised as I was with what had just happened. But he did his job of defending his client, I and my two members who assisted me just missed on what I thought was an airtight case. The victim identified her assailant plain and simple, and she could see clearly without her glasses. She used them more for reading.

I could not believe what I had just witnessed. I walked over to the witness box and explained to the victim what had just happened. She was most devastated. I tried to explain to her that crazy things happen in a court hearing. Her daughter, who also was present in the courtroom was also most devastated. She could not believe that justice was not served that day. She took her mother home.

BROWN was set free. A short time later, he was arrested in the West End area of Vancouver having just committed another rape. He was put in jail for that offence. I do not know what was, the final outcome, in that case, or what happened to Brown in his future life. I hoped he died in prison.

Chapter 34

CLIFFORD OLSEN - CANADA'S MASS MURDERER

Two of the members working on my unit came to me and told me that the suspect in a case I had assigned them to investigate and interrogate the suspect was likely involved in a more serious matter than originally thought. It was more than getting two young girls drunk and trying to assault them. He also appeared to have more going on than being a suspect in one sexual assault. He was a likely suspect in the disappearance of young girls, and boys from the surrounding Lower Mainland area of Vancouver. I advised my troop mate, Cpl Les FORSYTH, who happened to be in charge of other general criminal investigations to look into this suspect's background. Les went to work, and he started the investigation in what became the most dangerous sex murderer in Canadian history at the time.

The suspect was none other than the notorious, Clifford OLSEN. Apparently, OLSEN picked up the two young girls in Burnaby, and plied them with liquor while driving around the area. We later found out that he wanted to drop one of the young girls off, and take the other one with him; which he planned to have sex with her, and then kill her.

However, as he got the girls drunk, the one that he wanted to get out of the car, gave him such a bad time that he could not control her. She went berserk on him, and told him that he'd better drop both them off on the side of the road.

He got a bit concerned, and did just that, and then drove off. He apparently circled around the block to see what happened to them. It was a big mistake on his part, and a lucky break for us. The next car to drive past the girls was that of Cst. Quinton SMITH, in his marked police car. As he passed them, they started waving their hands, and yelling for him to stop. Quinton backed up to where the girls were and was getting the details of what these girls had encountered, just as the very curious OLSEN drove by. The girls pointed out the car to Quinton, who quickly pulled OLSEN over, and arrested him. OLSEN would not kill any more, young boys or girls.

I talked to one of the girls later about her encounter with OLSEN. The one thing that I recall is she was a very tough kid, and when she got drunk she became even more difficult to deal with. She said that some time back, she got into an argument with her mother, and it got quite physical when she shoved her arm through a window. She received a large gash in her arm, and there was blood all over. She was stitched up and recovered from the wounds. This did not slow her down, she could take on anybody, and that she did, as the notorious Clifford OLSEN found out. She should have gotten an award for her involvement in the capture of one of CANADA'S SERIAL KILLERS.

OLSEN was released. The RCMP put together a twenty-four-hour surveillance operation on OLSEN. He was eventually followed to Vancouver Island where he was observed to drive into someone's driveway, walk up to the house, and if it was unlocked, he walked in, and usually stole the woman's purse. This is quite often the case, as a lot of women leave their purse on a chair or staircase near the front door, and they become victims as in these situations.

Eventually OLSEN picked up a young female and did his usual liquor enticement by getting her drunk. He then drove into a wooded area where our members put him under arrest and saved a young female's life. OLSEN was interrogated, and an offer of $10,000 per dead victim was agreed upon, with OLSEN taking our members to places of where he'd murdered and dumped some of his victims. The rest is history, and a public record, is available on internet.

Chapter 35

TRAINING FOR VIP PROTECTION

I was selected for the RCMP training course for VIP PROTECTION which includes security protection for members of the Royal Family, prime ministers, presidents, heads of state of countries, and various other dignitaries. This involved more advanced driving, and shooting techniques, which we were not taught at the of time during our basic training course in Depot Division.

I had put on a new set of tires on an unmarked police car, (Chev Malibu), and off I went to the Boundary Bay Airport in Richmond B.C. This was the airport that was used to train pilots during the Second World War and had not been used as a regular working airport. The tarmac was pretty barren, with a few cracks in the pavement, but very functional for our use of driving at a high rate of speed in, and around the rubber orange cones which were set up in a strategic course. We got our instructions from our officers who drove us through the driving course at speeds of eighty to ninety miles an hour. The cars were sliding in, and out as we drove around the orange cones. It all seemed very exhilarating. I got very excited, and it perked up all my emotions, because I loved speed, which also had a downside, as I had to pay a few fines for my fun in my life. It was hard for me to slow down.

On one part of the course, I was hooked up with a partner, a senior S/Sgt from the RCMP Prince George Detachment. We had to monitor a section of where the orange cones were placed. As the cars went through this course some of the orange cones would get turned over from the wind currents, so we were to re-set the orange cones immediately, as within a few minutes, another car was coming through at about 85/100 mph, depending on the driver' capabilities.

The staff sergeant stayed at one section of the course, while I followed the speeding car off to one side to see if any of the orange cones got turned over, and if they did, I would quickly stop, and put them back in their position. I would be travelling about 85 to 95 mph., and if all the cones stayed in place I would turn around and return to where the staff sergeant was. On one instance, I saw that none of the cones was knocked over, so I stepped down on the emergency brake, turned my steering wheel to the left and went into a four-wheel drift sliding down the tarmac. As the car turned around, I immediately unlocked the emergency brake, turned the steering wheel to the right to straighten out the car, and stepped down hard on the gas pedal. With the rear wheels spinning rubber, all in a quick motion, I headed back to where the staff sergeant was standing. This manoeuvre was not part of our training course, but I had seen it done in the Hollywood movies.

I then realized that I might get disciplined by the senior staff sergeant for using the police vehicle in a reckless manoeuvre which was not part of our driving instructions. I drove up to where the staff sergeant was standing. He got into the passenger side of the car and was laughing loudly. He said that what I had done was amazing and that he wanted me to show him how it was done. So, I performed this maneuver a couple of times before the other candidates started coming down the racecourse.

Then I told him that we would switch positions so that he could try his ability in performing this manoeuvre. He said, "It's beyond my capabilities, I can go back to Prince George, and say I was in a car where this young member did this manoeuvre like in the movies."

The driving techniques were enjoyable, and we also had to back up through this twisted course at a very high rate of speed. "Faster the better" was what instructors told us.

Another part of this training course was the "instinctive shooting," which was not taught during our basic training in Depot Division. Targets were the usual policeman silhouette targets, which were placed at various distances. We were to fire our revolvers with two shots in a quick motion in the same place at the target. The manoeuvres were somewhat like a commando- style, crawling on the ground, turning around sometimes shooting at the target while lying down on your back. I was never in a situation during the rest of my service in the RCMP where I had to be confronted with this sort of thing.

Chapter 36

BOLIVAR MURDER INVESTIGATION

On November 23, 1982, the Burnaby RCMP detachment, received a bizarre call from some passers-by / walkers that they'd found the body of a dead woman on the side of the road leading up to the Horizon Restaurant on Burnaby Mountain. Our BBY General Duty members were first on the scene and secured the area. The Burnaby General Investigation Section was called in to handle the case.

I got involved in the investigation a few days later, when a number of residences needed to be kicked in (searched), and suspects taken into custody. I was assigned a townhouse residence next to where the victim (Mrs. Sharon BOLIVAR) was supposedly blindfolded, gagged, held against her will, mentally tortured, and then later driven to where she was executed. I had four junior RCMP members assigned to me. Some of them were from the General Duty Section and had not ever been exposed to a murder investigation, so this was a new beginning for them.

Prior to the assigned "kick in time", I debriefed my group of what we may encounter, and how we would respond to the threats.

At roughly 06:00 hours, my group would kick in our assigned residence, while the other group of investigators would simultaneously kick in the adjoining townhouse. I had one of the strongest, muscular constables of the Burnaby detachment, named Doug DZORKO. So, I assigned him to take the sledgehammer, and smash the doorknob, then we would kick the door in. Well, the best laid plans can also go wrong. We walked up quietly to the front door of the residence, as Doug prepared to swing the sledgehammer. Then with all his might, he swung the sledgehammer, only to miss the doorknob, and bury the sledgehammer into the door. By now the family dog had gotten involved and started barking. The scene became a bit laughable for a brief moment. I then moved Doug aside and kicked in the door. Constable Scott FILER was first to enter and stumbled over the dog and fell down. I went in immediately, revolver in my right hand, ready for action. My flashlight was on and I ran down a hallway past a bedroom where a young boy half stood up from his sleep in his bed, crying, and screaming. I went farther down the hallway and entered a bedroom. I shone my flashlight on a man, and woman in bed. The man started to reach for his rifle. I shouted at him "RCMPOLICE, don't move, hands up, you're under arrest for murder of Sharon BOLIVAR". My guys quickly put the cuffs on him, and we made them get out of bed, and moved them into their living room.

I immediately went into the hysterical kid's bedroom. I tried to calm him down, then I told him to join his mom in the living room. She told me it was his birthday that day. What bad timing. I immediately got hold of one of our uniform constables and hoped that a ride in a police car might cheer him up. His mother was helpful and told him that they would meet him at the police office. I gave the uniform constable some money for a MacDonald's meal and told him to buy whatever the child wanted - within reason of course.

We put the couple in separate cars and drove them to the detachment. I interviewed the woman first. She immediately told me that her husband was a friend of the Allan RODNEY, the driver of the car that had taken the woman to her execution spot. RODNEY told her husband who did what in this murder. She was very scared, because RODNEY's friends who did the killing were really dangerous. I assured her not to worry, said that, if she and her husband cooperated there would be no way that the ones responsible for the murder would get out of jail.

I then interviewed the husband, who at first would not tell me anything. I told him it was up to him if he wanted to go to jail with his friends, but his time was running out. His child would grow up knowing who he was associated with - in this case "one of the gang" of murderers. I told him if he cooperated, then he would not be charged as he did not appear to be part of the murder plot. He did not take long to think about it, but was very concerned about SPEICHER, who executed Sharon BOLIVAR. He told me SPEICHER was unforgiving, and was a real cold-blooded killer, and a very dangerous person. I told him not to worry. He then related all what he knew of what RODNEY told him surrounding the murder of Sharon BOLIVAR.

At this time, Cpl. Lloyd PLANTE, and Cpl. Rick LAWRENCE were continuing their interrogation of the real murderer in this case, SPEICHER. Some of the details of the interrogation methods by myself, and others came into dispute later. There were a lot of mixed emotions going on, as some felt this victim could have been their wife, sister, mother, or their best friend. They wanted the murderers to feel the pain.

By now it was running late in the day. Other members tried interviewing RODNEY, but he would not tell them anything. I went into the interview room where he was being held. I started to talk to him, and he was being his arrogant self, and at one point he kind of fell asleep. I kicked the chair away that he was sitting in and grabbed him bodily before he hit the floor. I threw him up against the wall with one my hands at his throat. He was now fully alert. I looked him in the eyes and told him that I was going to take him to where they executed Mrs. BOLIVAR and I was going to kill him. He looked surprised and did not know what to make of what I had just told him. I left him in the room and got constables Steve BERNEY and Rod MacDONALD and told them to blind-fold RODNEY and tell him that they were taking him to where he drove BOLIVAR. I also advised BERNEY and MacDONALD that I would be with constable Dave FINNEN in the bush area near where the execution was committed. They were to take RODNEY (still blindfolded) out of the car and tell him that we were going to kill him and make him kneel, down. At that point, FINNEN and I would provide the gunshots in the bush and hope to startle RODNEY's memory of the murder. Apparently, RODNEY was not believing what was happening to him, so he started screaming. FINNEN fired the first shot from his 38 cal. police revolver. It did not make a loud noise as I thought it would. I immediately took out my .357 cal. Magnum Smith & Wesson revolver and fired two quick shots into a tree. (This was an illegal firearm, not a RCMP-issued revolver. I purchased it after I was involved in a gunfight in April 1979, where I almost got my head shot off). The shots were so loud that even FINNEN was startled. I felt it had the impressive shock effect.

BERNEY and MacDONALD took RODNEY back to the detachment, and I was told that RODNEY gave his version of what happened in the murder plot.

Well, the next day, we got the bad news, that our interrogation technique had hit the news. We (the BBY RCMP had taken the murder suspect back to the scene of the crime, and shot at him, but we let him live). Glen ORRIS, a well-known criminal defence lawyer complained about not getting to see his clients, the murder suspects. Apparently, Cpl. Lloyd PLANTE, at the time would not let ORRIS see his client, for whatever reasons.

I thought it would be best if I had a meeting with Supt. Norm FUCHS, I/C of the Burnaby Detachment. He was not a fan of some of the plain clothes members in the General Investigation Section, but I had a good working relationship with Supt. FUCHS. At that time, I was a staff representative for the BBY RCMP members, junior to the officer (inspector) rank down, and would assist them in any disputes they may have with senior members, etc. I would attend the monthly meetings with FUCHS, and admin staff on detachment matters. When I attended my first detachment admin meeting, Supt. FUCHS told me that I did not have a vote on matters which was the norm for the previous staff representative. After a few monthly meetings, Supt. FUCHS, changed his mind, and asked my opinion on the matters being discussed. I now had a voice of influence, so to speak. So when this matter hit the news media, and with the respect that I had for Supt FUCHS, I thought it was my duty to have a meeting with him. I immediately went to see FUCHS. I told him that I was the one who put things in motion and the other members should not suffer the consequences of this interrogation technique.

Supt. FUCHS put on a pleasant face and said to me, " Merv, the general public has been phoning me nonstop, and wondering why when we took the murderer back to the scene of the crime, that we did not kill him as that was what should have happened. The public are backing us and are in full support of your actions. You put us on the map, so to speak. I would like to remind you of the Nuremberg Trials. The generals all said that they were following HITLER'S orders, but that did not exclude them from not being guilty of their crimes. They were willing participants. Do not say anything further. Go back and advise all your members who are involved, that we will get you good lawyers, as required by our regulations. This will eventually blow over. Emotions run high."

We shook hands, and l left his office, with a good feeling that he had our backs. My heartfelt respect for Supt. FUCHS remained throughout my service. He was a private man of sorts which carried through to his retirement, and when he died, it was no surprise that he requested no service.

Five of us BBY GIS members were charged under the RCMP ACT for "conduct unbecoming a member of the RCMP". We were also charged criminally for assault and intimidation. All of us appeared in the presence of Asst/Commissioner VENNER where he commented that he had never assembled all five RCMP members together for the official warning. The usual RCMP procedure is for each member to be tried, and served a warning, etc., separately. He said that this was an unusual case, where the general public did not want us charged. However, the RCMP must be seen to be upholding their high police standards. He thanked us for doing a commendable job in solving this crime.

The RCMP hired five top criminal lawyers in Vancouver for each one of us. My lawyer was Joe WOOD. I met with him, and we discussed my case. Within a couple of weeks, he called me and said that he had been appointed as a Judge to the BC SUPREME COURT, and he could no longer take on my case. However, if I was in agreement he would pass my case to Dave GIBBONS, a partner in his law firm. He would brief GIBBONS on what strategy we would take in my defence. I agreed with that. I felt that I had a good defence team, as I could not go wrong with a judge of the BC SUPREME COURT, assisting his partner in handling my case. It proved to be the right move. We went through a brief preliminary hearing, and eventually GIBBONS, and the crown counsel decided there was inefficient evidence to proceed. So, these murderers, RODNEY in my case, could not make the charges stick so as a result, I was absolved of the criminal charges.

SPEICHER was later found to be responsible for a couple of murders in Ontario. Once SPEICHER's name became public, and was spread across the media, the BBY detachment got a call from a man living on Vancouver Island saying he was present about a year prior to SPEICHER 's arrest, when SPEICHER shot a man in his presence during a drug deal that went bad. He was scared of SPEICHER, as he said SPEICHER was a very dangerous man, and he waited until SPEICHER was in custody before he would notify the RCMP of the murder. He took our GIS members to the crime scene where they found the human remains. These human remains were identified as one of Sgt. Don WILKIE's, Vancouver Drug Squad's informants. WILKIE was wondering why he had not been able to contact him for so long.

All the other members had their charges stayed. SPEICHER and his associate, Merrill Carson KEVILL were sentenced to life in prison. RODNEY was sentenced to sixteen years for his involvement in the BOLIVAR murder. All three murderers were beaten up in prison shortly after their arrival in gaol.

A few years later, our crown prosecutor in this case had been diagnosed with a brain tumour that was inoperable, and he died a short time later. RODNEY appealed his sentence a few years later and was given more time in prison. He was sentenced to life in prison. SPEICHER within a few years in prison got inoperable cancer. He wanted to be transferred to a prison in Ontario, so he could be close to his family. He was advised by the Correctional Centre authorities that they would not move him, and he was told that he would be buried in a cold grave at the Prince Albert Correctional Centre.

A few years later, I was retired from the RCMP, and at the Vancouver Supreme Court House on another matter, when I ran into Glen ORRIS, who was on another case. Glen, being a first class, gentleman, said he wanted to apologize to me, as somehow the media had gotten wind of this story about my interrogation methods, and confronted him outside the entrance to the Burnaby detachment. He just spoke out of what he knew of the excessive force we used on these murderers. He felt that the media story no doubt caused me a lot of stress, and may have affected my job, etc. I accepted his apologies and told him that it was water under the bridge, so to speak. I was able to take it as part of my character, and the excitement I had in the RCMP. So this story ended.

Chapter 37

SCARING THE LIFE OUT OF MY PARTNER

One evening what we thought was going to be a quiet night turned out nothing of the sort. I was driving our police cruiser in north Burnaby and was accompanied by the next zone commander Cpl Leif OLSEN. As things seemed quiet in the northern Burnaby area, so we thought we would drive around together, using one car instead of two, and we would cover whatever was required (conscience of public tax dollars).

Then we got a call that there was a fight at the Admiral Hotel, which was the watering hole for the outlaw motorcycle gang members and criminals alike. One of my constables got thrown through a plate glass window and got cut up. Cpl Leif OLSEN and I raced down Hastings St. I was driving, and as I have had the VIP training in high speed defensive driving, I took Leif on a wild ride of his life. We were travelling somewhere between 85/100 mph, with all the emergency equipment activated. Leif got a little nervous, we were now in God's hands driving his gas guzzling chariot. What a ride. Whew!!!

The sirens were blaring. As we neared the Admiral Hotel, I braked hard, tires were screaming, I turned the car to the left, and we were sliding down the pavement in a four- wheel drift. The crowd saw us coming, and they started to scatter. I scared the crowd, and some of them made a run for it, as we came to a stop. Leif jumped out of the car, and both of us immediately ended up in a major fight with the bad guys.

I grabbed two guys by their necks, and then put them in a choke hold. I tried to choke them out and subdue them, but I was having a difficult time. I was able to see our wounded member near where he got injured. Leif was battling with a couple of guys, and one guy was trying to steal his revolver. I let go of one of the guys and pulled the bad guy off Leif. I managed to grab the other guy in a head lock so he could not steal Leif's revolver. I left myself wide open, because out of nowhere came a solid fist to my nose, and then I saw stars.

The bad guys grabbed their two guys off me. I ended up with a sore bloody nose. The guy who hit me, grabbed my police hat, and ran like the DICKENS. I am sure "THIS HAT" is on someone's mantelpiece as a souvenir, if that person is still alive.

Bad guys sometimes do not have a long-life span. BBY Det called the Vancouver City Police for back up, they came within a few minutes of our arrival. They arrived speeding eastbound along Hastings St. Some of the crowd started to run, others remained defiant including a tough woman in high heels, (a " broad," as we said in those times). She started kicking Leif. I grabbed her, threw her aside, and grabbed another bad guy. The city cops came, and they started beating the hell out of the bad guys, who ended up being thrown into the paddy wagon.

We made a number of arrests. Our wounded member, Cst Quinton SMITH was taken to emergency, and got patched up. He did not have any life-threatening injuries, thank God!

Well, this was one of those fun stories for the coffee room, and beer drinking parties. This is quite common for the Vancouver

Police and BBY RCMP to assist in each other's barroom battles, or whenever further assistance is required. We were dealing with the same assholes, so the general policy was to go to the other police jurisdiction and beat the hell out of the bad guys. Inflict as much, injuries to them as possible, then get quickly back in your police car, and take off. Nobody could remember who hit whom.

Chapter 38

MEETING MY WIFE

I met a young beautiful woman who lived in West Vancouver and later became my second wife. I had already bought a house in New Westminster, Queens Park area, from the proceeds of my divorce settlement, and was quite comfortable living there. There were not that many older single members to party around with, so it was not common for NCO's and constables to party around with the officer rank of the RCMP. However, there was a single, divorced inspector, who liked to party around. So, I got to know him, although he was not my supervisor, which was a good thing. We became friends and he was my best man when Caroline and I got married.

Inspector (later Superintendent), Bob BYAM was a character that was a bit on the wild side, and he was a lot of fun. So my future wife Caroline, lined Bob up with a couple of her girlfriends. We went out on several double dates and had a great time. Back to business, Bob had a good friend in our staffing branch, and was influential to get me transferred to the North Vancouver

Detachment, which was what I wanted. It was closer to where Caroline lived.

Within a few months, through love and agreement, I moved into Caroline's house, and rented out my house in New Westminster. It was going to be a new experience for me, as Caroline had two young daughters, a seventeen-year-old, and a thirteen-year-old.

My position at the North Vancouver Detachment was to handle the numerous problems with house parties, and general liquor violations, which seemed to have gotten out of hand in the North Vancouver District. This was a plain clothes position, for which I was OK with. A few months later I got involved in assisting the North Vancouver Detachment General Duty members with a rowdy house party. They got a call from a young resident that he wanted people removed from his house. Upon opening the door of the house, I encountered Samantha, Caroline's oldest daughter, with a beer in her hand, crouching down under the armpits of some tall drunk young men, who were not concerned about my presence. I told her to get out of the house as fast as she could, as I was bringing in a bunch of guys, and we were throwing every-one out.

She immediately disappeared within the house. I ordered the members in. We ended up fighting our way in, and eventually cleared out the house, and shoved the rowdy people up the street. There was some chatter among the party people about my name being mentioned amongst them, which the general duty members overheard. They later told me that they were surprised that I was so well known, as I had recently arrived at the North Van Det. Maybe my reputation followed me from BURNABY whereby I had ordered our riot team to bust up a house party there a few months ago.

Chapter 39

MEETING A HELL'S ANGELS MEMBER

After a few months, I was put in charge of the North Vancouver NCIS (National Crime Intelligence Section). It was two-man unit, with Cst. Bob WOOLF as my partner. He was a humorous, senior constable, who had a drinking, and a gambling problem. There was not too much happening in relation to national crime at the detachment, other than monitoring a few members of the Hells Angels motorcycle club members.

One member of the club decided to apply for a FAC (Firearm Acquisition Permit), which was quite a surprise. Supt. Roy BRYNE, i/c of the North Vancouver Detachment told me that it was his wish that I do not approve the permit; however, it was my department's responsibility, and it was entirely up to me if I wanted to approve it. I thought it over, as I knew this biker's background. A few years prior, he and two other Hells Angels members kicked (murdered) a bouncer to death at one of the Vancouver city night clubs. He got off from these charges as the Hell's Angels threatened the female witness that he would kill her if she testified against them. She changed her story, and the Vancouver City Police were not able to proceed with the murder charges. I called the biker and had him come to the Detachment.

I had Cst. WOOLF set up in the North Vancouver Fire Department building across the street from the entrance to the detachment, so he could get some new photos of the biker. When I met the biker in the lobby, he told me that he knew he was being photographed. I smiled and told him we would be watching him more closely from then on out as I was going to give him his permit.

I also told him that I knew of his past character, and if an opportunity came to us, whereby we had information to kick in his door, that I would come, and kill him. He said that I could not do that. I said that I now knew that he had a permit for his shotgun, which I was giving him, and I very well knew his character of beating, and killing people in the past. He took the permit and left. It was a short while later, that he moved out of his house, and took up residence outside of North Vancouver.

My partner, Bob WOOLF, was quite a guy, and full of fun. He had some issues that consumed his life. He liked his liquor, and he liked to gamble. There were times that he would come to work with the smell of liquor on his breath. I would quickly suggest to him that we better get in our car, and check out, or do some surveillance on some of our suspects that we were working on, in case he came into contact with other office staff. He would tell me that he had had about a couple of hours of sleep, because his baby daughter kept him awake. I found out later from one of the uniform members that several members were at his house that evening and were gambling until late evening hours. This eventually led to marital and financial problems.

Bob eventually sold his house and moved into rental accommodations. One day he had a physical altercation with his wife and lost his temper. He pulled out his service revolver and threatened her with it. She left the house with their child. Bob spent the rest of the day consuming a lot of liquor. Later that evening, things got out of hand. Bob was outside his rental apartment not far from the North Vancouver Detachment, acting in a very disturbing manner, with his revolver in his hand. An RCMP member, and good friend of his tried to talk to him and get him to drop his revolver. Bob did what no one wants to witness. He pointed his revolver at his head and pulled the trigger. I visit his gravesite at the Capilano View Cemetery, whenever I am there paying my respects to my mother-in-law, and a young woman, Christine MISARYAN, who was tragically murdered in Washington DC in 1998. Christine's parents are good friends of Caroline's and mine. There is another story surrounding Christine's death.

Chapter 40

SHAKING HANDS WITH CLINT EASTWOOD

Caroline and I decided to take a summer holiday to California. We went on a wine tour of the Napa Valley and stayed at some accommodations somewhere near Monterey. I heard that Clint EASTWOOD, the famous movie actor/producer had a restaurant, the HOGS BREATH INN, somewhere in Carmel, where he was the mayor.

We eventually found the restaurant and were able to get in despite not having made any dinner reservations. We asked the host/hostess if this was Clint EASTWOOD's restaurant, and if he'd make an appearance that evening. They said it was his restaurant and he came in now and then, and it was hit and miss, but we may be lucky. We ordered our dinner, and were near finishing it, when I noticed Clint EASTWOOD walking in.

I said to Caroline, "Guess who walked in?" She asked who it was, and I told her Clint had just walked in. He walked over to the bar and was standing up talking to the bartender. All of a sudden, two hot-to-trot middle aged women got up from their table and walked over to the bar. I guess they were going to hit on Clint, who was having no part in their game. We finished our dinner and paid our bill.

I could not leave the restaurant without saying hello to Mr. Clint EASTWOOD. I tried my luck, and I did not want to bother him. So, I walked up to him, and said, "Pardon me, Mr. EASTWOOD, we drove all the way from Vancouver to visit your restaurant and we enjoyed it. Thank you very much." I put out my hand. He shook my hand and said, "Thanks and glad you enjoyed it. Have a nice vacation." I said, "You made my day." He smiled and we both had a little laugh. It was a conversation line from his movie *DIRTY HARRY*. This was where he pointed his .44 cal. Magnum revolver at the criminal he was chasing, and when he had him cornered, he said, "MAKE MY DAY."

Chapter 41

AIR INDIA BOMBING

It was June 23, 1985, when a bomb exploded, and sent an Air India 747 jetliner Flight #182 from Vancouver down into the Atlantic Ocean near Cork, Ireland, killing 329 innocent victims. Another bomb explosion at Narita, Japan, blew up in the airport killing two baggage handlers, who were taking luggage out of another Air India jet liner that also came from Vancouver.

About a year later, I was transferred to our Air India Bombing Task Force. Within a few months after my arrival, the RCMP and CSIS (the Canadian spy agency) were having some personnel, and political problems, particularly with the exchange of very sensitive information.

Some of the CSIS members, who were former members of the RCMP, now selected me to be the RCMP liaison officer to CSIS.

I found out later the reason for my selection was I had the right temperament, and both parties got along with me.

My duty/ responsibility was to meet with, my counterpart, Al JONES, (a former member of the RCMP) now a CSIS agent, at his office, and read all pertinent secret documents, coming from various Intelligence Agencies (UK, USA, various European Nations, India), and forward what I thought was pertinent for enforcement regarding any terrorist's activities in Canada. JONES, in his position attended at my office, and would read all documents, reports, etc., that were pertinent to the CSIS mandate.

Shortly after these arrangements were made, the Commonwealth Heads Of Government (CHOGM) scheduled their meeting to take place in Vancouver in October, 1987. This was shortly after the Air India bombing when there was a great concern about the safety of some of the heads of states. The potential targets for terrorists were 1) Prime Minister Margaret THATCHER of the United Kingdom, the IRA's number-one target, 2) Prime Minister Rajiv GANDHI of India, Sikhs' number-one target throughout the world.

Supt. Lyman HENSCHEL, was the overall security commander for CHOGM. He called me into his office, and told me that if anything went wrong, my head, and Al JONES's head would be the first ones to roll, as we were the first line of information. We were reading these various documents, and passing on what we thought was pertinent to various police departments for enforcement, etc. This is where things could go wrong in our interpretation of information that was gleaned from these secret documents, and then by not passing them on for enforcements, etc. What may surprise a lot of people, is that the security (information only, in this respect) for this event came down to my counterpart in CSIS, and a low-level police officer, a Corporal (ME). It was mostly my responsibility because of police enforcement. We kept it together, and there were no security problems.

I worked long hours and did not get much sleep. I also took work home, so I could read some information and take care of business. I was never so relieved when the meeting was over, and then it was "wheels up". As soon as we got word that Prime Minster THATCHER was in her Concord Jetliner, and Prime Minister Rajiv GANDHI was in his 747, and both were in international air space, we had a little celebration. A lot of us were having a good time at our RCMP watering hole.

Sikh terrorists were quite active during this period in India, as well as in Canada, and other countries throughout the world. They stirred up their hate for the Indian government. They did anything to disrupt, or cause damage, or financial loss for the Indian government. It was a short life for PM Rajiv GANDHI, as he was killed in a bomb explosion in India on May 21, 1991. His mother, Prime Minister Indra GANDHI was also assassinated previously on October 31,1984 in India, which was a result of her government's raid on the Sikhs' GOLDEN TEMPLE in Amritsar. PM Margaret THATCHER, survived to live on to her natural death (dementia) in 2013.

Chapter 42

TRANSFER TO SUPPORT SERVICES

Shortly after CHOGM, I was offered a career move to the Support Services Section, responsible for media relations and other duties. I was working for one of the favourite, capable, senior commanders in the RCMP, Supt Lyman HENSCHEL, and I was looking forward to a possible promotion.

However, bureaucracy has its problems. Just before my transfer to Support Services, an "Asshole Sgt. BW (name withheld for certain reasons)", from my previous position on the Air India Task Force was responsible in writing up my yearly performance evaluation. He downgraded my score which put me out for the selection process for the sergeant's promotion.

While I was on the National Security Task Force, and was responsible for handling sensitive information, our Senior Management said that I had to report to Chief Superintendent Frank PALMER, thereby passing the NCO ranks of Sergeant, Staff Sergeant, and Senior Officer ranks of Inspector and Superintendent. Perhaps this caused some jealousy along the way.

In one particular instance, around 3:30 p.m., just before everyone was ending their shift, Sgt. BW decided to get a group of his favourite members who were on the Task Force and go on a surveillance of an Indian male that was a very vaguely suspect in the Air India bombing. This was putting all these members on overtime hours, hence earning them extra money which I felt was definitely not warranted. It was a bit of corruption on Sergeant BW's part as a supervisor. I told him that from my information, this was not warranted, and as from my reading of secret documents surrounding this person, he was not a suspect or target that they should go after, thus wasting tax dollars. Sgt. BW got annoyed and called off this surveillance. This no doubt played into his downgrading my evaluation. I discussed this later with C/Supt. PALMER, who eventually apologized. I was reporting to him, so he should have completed my annual performance evaluation, but the damage had been done.

I recall PALMER exhibiting signs of having very severe headaches, when I went into his office to discuss certain aspects of the sensitive information that I was dealing with. I asked him if he was OK, and he told he was having severe headaches. Ironically, there was another CSIS agent who was going through the same mental problem. This no doubt played into PALMER pushing off doing my annual evaluation to Sergeant BW, who most likely wanted to write it up.

I had written up the job description for the Media Liaison Section, which I was requested to do, and that it was to be upgraded from a Corporal to a Sergeant's position, with this supported by Supt. HENSCHEL. I had been performing these duties for about a year, so everyone thought I should have gotten the promotion. However, that did not happen.

Deputy Commissioner Don WILSON actually phoned me to apologize for not being able to interfere or change the promotional process. He had been able to do that for other members in the past; however, our HQ in Ottawa had recently changed the rules for the promotional process, and I became a casualty of the system.

Chapter 43

MY LAST JOB IN THE RCMP

With my experience in major crime investigations, undercover operations, and CSIS liaison, the RCMP offered me a position in our National Criminal Information Analytical Section which I accepted. It involved a lot of reading documents, or complaints to glean whether a crime had been committed, and who the participants were, and their involvement. A lot of this was done using the auto-cad computer (used by engineers and draftsmen for their work) to make flow charts, etc.

One of my first projects was the involvement/corruption by a MLA member of the New Democratic Party of British Columbia. I was handed a number of documents about a foot and a half high, which I had to read through, and decipher who did what with the particular party donations. I was told that the RCMP were to come up with some concrete information within two or three weeks. I started reading, and made several charts documenting various individuals as to what they did with the money, etc. I could not get it done within that time frame, as there was a lot to read, and I had to rest my mind at times. I completed the work in roughly about a month and a half. It was the largest organizational chart I had ever done. In the end, I was quite satisfied with the results, which made it easier for our investigators to do their work. When they completed their investigation, this MLA, and some of his associates in the NDP were found to be taking money for their own use, in violation of election standards for the government.

Chapter 44

DINNER MEETING WITH PHILIPPINES PRESIDENT FERDINAND MARCOS'S FINANCIAL ADVISOR

One evening my wife, Caroline and I were invited to a dinner party held at an acquaintance's (name changed to Dan & Marge), house in Southlands, a very upscale area of Vancouver. This was a very palatial house on a bit of acreage with riding stables on it. The hosts were very friendly, which made me somewhat guarded "due to my being" in the RCMP.

We originally met Dan and Marge when Caroline's school friend from Calcutta India, Ester and her husband Matty, and their family came to visit us the summer previously. Ester contacted Marge, and the friendship began. Ester being of the Jewish faith eventually left India, moved to Israel, and married Matty who worked for El Al Airlines. Their family endured several bombing incidents committed by the Palestinians. Ester and Matty knew Marge in Israel before she moved to CANADA and corresponded with her over the years. It is a small world. Ester, who hates flying, worked up the courage, and decided to travel to Vancouver, and visit her friends. Incidentally, Caroline and I took a Mediterranean cruise after we got engaged in 1984, and had a day stopover in Haifa, Israel. We briefly met Ester and Matty, who drove us around their small country. It was then that Caroline, and Ester caught up with the latest news of friends, etc. We got to see a number of the historical sites, such as "THE VIA DOLOROSA," latin translation for "SORROWFUL WAY". That is where JESUS dragged the cross to his faithful end. I could not imagine the horrific pain HE went through. The rest is history.

Back to the party, we had cocktails served up by some of their catering staff in their living room. It was a marvellous party. The host showed us around his new house, which was quite impressive with two marble fountains with water trickling down a statue. One was located at the outside entrance, and another one was located inside the house immediately as you entered through the front door. The hostess was of the Jewish faith and had been born and brought up in Iraq. I believe she may have had some connections to India, perhaps it was her reason to make friends with Caroline, as that was where Caroline was also born and grew up. The hostess was over the top, and she had this unusual high-pitched voice, which was quite captivating after being in her company for some time.

There was a special guest of honour, that the host and hostess were fussing about. He happened to be the financial advisor (phonetic name, Dooie Go Dee,) to the president of the Philippines, Ferdinand MARCOS. MARCOS's wife, Imelda, was quite well known around the world as an extravagant shopper and had a collection of shoes beyond one's imagination. There was a scandal surrounding MARCOS's government with widespread corruption, etc., and that money had been taken out of the country, and put in Swiss Bank accounts, and elsewhere. Dooie arranged for the money transfers, etc., and left the country as he became the "wanted man", by the new government. He came to Canada with his family and was being protected by all the diplomatic bureau-cracy. I suspected that Dooie had laundered some money through connections in Canada, and therein lay where secrets abounded, and my interest of all the people at this party. I appreciated the dinner invite we had received from our hosts, and I got to do some spying, etc.

The time came for us to have dinner. We were escorted into this large dining room that had a large table set for twenty-four guests. We each had a special place to sit. I was placed next to Dooie's wife, who was quite charming. The conversation was not guarded, and she spoke openly about things in the Philippines, and that they were very happy now living in Canada. I did not elaborate on my knowledge of their circumstances being in Canada, and I knew that Field Marshall RAMOS, MARCOS's top military commander was our Informant, so to speak. A very twisted, seedy world we live in. Sometimes you have to make a deal with the devil.

I eventually got a chance to briefly talk to Dooie, while he was sitting quietly in one part of the living room. He had a medical health problem of gout, commonly referred to as, "a rich man's illness." I asked him about his life in the Philippines, and if he experienced some violence during his association with MARCOS. He knew I was in the RCMP, obviously briefed by the host and hostess. He told me about one time when he was being driven to MARCOS's palace, and they were using two vehicles, with blackened-out windows, one of which was a decoy vehicle. They came under machine gun fire, and he was slightly wounded. They escaped, and he moved to Canada shortly thereafter. He had a dif-ficult time with his speech, perhaps due to his medical issue.

I asked Dooie if he thought things were better under President AQUINO's Government, than when he was there. He said that nothing changed, just the players changed. In other words there were new people in charge of taking the government's money and doing very little for the population. He said, "Change happens when blood flows in the street. In order to change things, blood must flow in the street." I thought that was a very profound statement as you look throughout history, and in present political situations in various parts of the world where there is a lot of corruption. There are blood baths between rival political parties, whereby change happens, not always for the good.

We have been invited several times to this family residence, and they were all grand performances. Caroline wanted to carry on this friendship, so we had them over to our place for a party with a much smaller crowd. I had seen that their residence started to come under a bit of a decay, with water leaks. I suspected this came from the cheap unqualified labour they used in building. They always talked about the bargains, and the great deals they got in association with their business. The hostess always talked about wanting to get her various friends, including us, into some sort of businesses. I just never got involved, as I could see this going over the cliff before long.

Unfortunately, their business suffered a loss, then they moved residences. Their oldest daughter married a Jewish fellow from California whom the hostess wanted me to check out. I told her I was unable to do this. The family moved briefly to California and decided to live periodically in both countries. The eldest daughter had a child and remained in the USA. Dan was later diagnosed with brain cancer and died shortly thereafter. He was a nice gentleman, and it was sad that this happened to him. We had lost contact with them for a period in time and kept them as a distance friendship. Recently we connected with them for a few lunches, during a visit from Ester's sister from Israel. We had a very brief discussion about the political situation, which I have a great appetite for.

We visited Israel in the past, and saw the Golan Heights, the Dead Sea, Jerusalem, Bethlehem, and various historical sites. It is a very interesting place to see, and well worth a visit for everyone. Interesting to note, is that the various Christian churches have a different perspective on Jesus's final moment on this earth!!!!

Chapter 45

MEETING PRESIDENT VLADIMIR PUTIN

One of my extra duties while working at DCIAS (division criminal information analytical section) was to perform security duties for visiting dignitaries to Canada. April 4, 1993 was the date set for USA President Bill CLINTON to have a Summit Meeting with his Russian counterpart, President Boris YELTSIN. Vancouver was the chosen location, and we had three weeks to plan all the security arrangements.

Usually there would be one trained RCMP member for each of VIP's required responsibilities; however, they ran out of trained available members in Vancouver to do the job when they came to the health services category. I was advised that I had to handle the responsibilities for both presidents. I laboured long hours, to put my plan together, and then I was advised that the Russians were sending out their pre-boarding party a week ahead of the designated date.

This was about the time the West (USA, UK, FRANCE, GERMANY, CANADA, Other allied countries) were trying to accept the USSR (particularly Russia) which was now trying to embrace the Western way of life. I was to meet the Russian security delegation at the Pan Pacific Hotel. I was in the last stages of my security plan and had to get the final details typed out. However, I went ahead to meet President YELTSIN's doctor.

I entered the designated Pan Pacific Hotel boardroom and found that the RUSSIAN KGB were sitting on one side of the table and on the opposite side, the RCMP, US SECRET SERVICE, and FBI had assembled. Everybody appeared to have questionable looks on their faces. A quick look on the KGB faces, said it all. After all, we had kicked the KGB agents out of Canada, and they had kicked our agents out in the past, and now we were trying to get along. The Russians had just been beaten and suffered a lot of casualties in their conflict in Afghanistan. The Americans had their own problems with the Russians, but now the Cold War was supposedly over, and we, the West were trying to welcome the Commies, (former USSR republics, etc) into our way of life.

I decided to break the ice, and said in the Ukrainian language, "How do you do?" I figured that some of these KGB guys understood Ukrainian or recognized the language. This would be a pretty common greeting in the Slavic countries. The KGB agents remained stone faced, while the RCMP, and some of FBI and the Secret Service uttered some small laughter. They picked up on my humour. I also wanted to send some doubt to the KGB agents that I might have an understanding of their language and put them on edge a bit.

I was then introduced to President YELTSIN's doctor, who spoke English, and who was friendly, and was standing near the KGB table. I took him aside, and we left the conference room. I said I would take him to see the arrangements that I made for any upcoming problems that President YELTSIN may experience. For all the reports I read, and viewing news clips, I suspected Boris had an alcoholic/drinking problem. Some previous TV clips showed him dancing. He appeared to be a bit tipsy. I asked the doctor how

President YELTSIN's health was, and I got the usual brave answer that he was in great shape. I expected that; however, I suspected he may have some heart problems. So, I had made pre-arrangements with the medical personnel at St. PAUL's HOSPITAL.

I took YELTSIN's doctor to meet the cardiologist, who was most eager, and did an excellent job describing the procedure, etc, and showed him such modern equipment, and in the most modern facilities. We actually saw some heart patients coming out of the operating room. I was very impressed myself.

We returned to the PAN PACIFIC HOTEL, where YELTSIN's doctor took me into one secure room where I saw the KGB setting up their equipment. There was a female KGB agent, who looked more like a hooker, and had a lot of miles on her. Also in the room was a pretty solid, tall male KGB agent, who's body language showed me that he was not impressed that the doctor brought me into the room. They exchanged some conversation that I did not understand, so I told the KGB agents that I needed them to provide me with a Russian translator as they would not trust ours. I told them I will need one before the visit got under way, and they assured me that they would get me one. I said goodbye to the doctor and told him I would be in touch. I felt that he had a good feeling that WILD BORIS would be in excellent hands. I went back to finish the final details of my security plan.

A few days later, with the Summit Conference in progress at the University of British Columbia Museum of Anthropology where PRESIDENT's CLINTON & YELTSIN & PRIME MINSTER BRIAN MULRONEY were having their meeting, I noticed the KGB agents were grouped together near their Russian limo, while the RCMP, US SECRET SERVICE, FBI and Vancouver Police Department were gathered in another area.

I felt I would break the ice a bit, so I walked over to the KGB agents, and asked if anybody could speak English. A shorter male agent about my age said he spoke English. I said, "Welcome to Canada.", and shook his hand. I then asked him, "We are wondering, with you coming from a communist political system, trying to change, to have a democratic government system, would you ever go back to the communist way of life?" This guy said, "No, the older population wants to hold onto the communist way of life, but the younger people want what you have - blue jeans, cars, night clubs, etc." He then said, "We are open for business, we have mini submarines for sale." I looked at him with a bit of interest and was curious about the mini submarines. He said, "We take the armaments out, and these subs could be used for tourism in underwater exploration."

I did not know they had mini submarines; however, the Japanese had them during the Second World War, so why wouldn't the Soviets have them? I told him that I was near retirement, would check around, and might be able to find someone that would be interested in them. He said, "A friend of mine is an Admiral in charge of the BLACK SEA FLETT." I figured this guy was very connected, first having a friend who is an Admiral, top rank in the navy, and in charge of the Black Sea Fleet, but was not sure where their base was. So, I asked him for a contact person, and got him to write it down in my notebook. I believe he wrote either the admiral's name, or the name his other (spy), and a phone number in Moscow, as well as a phone number of their Soviet/Russian embassy in Ottawa. I was called away, as I had to go to another venue where the delegation would be meeting and had to make sure my people were in place as per my security plan. I did not get his name. I checked my notebook that I had stored away upon my retirement, and there are the phone numbers, and a name.

The Summit Conference went off without any problems.

I thought about getting us (RCMP) together with CSIS, the FBI, CIA, other Intelligence Agencies involved in secretly phoning the Moscow phone number from our secure phone line and have a conversation with the person in Moscow. If this was PUTIN OR PUTIN's CONTACT PERSON, they would most likely want to invite me to Moscow. They would know that I was in the RCMP, and once I was in their country, they might want to recruit me to be their spy/informant on things of their interest. They could also have me arrested as a SPY and use me for bargaining on any events regarding espionage. ESPIONAGE would have been exciting, and also very dangerous, and I felt I had done my bit for this country and was considering retirement.

In 1991, WILD PRESIDENT BORIS YELTSIN was elected president of the Russian Soviet Federal Socialist Republic. YELTSIN was having problems functioning as a leader. He was eventually ousted out and replaced by VLADIMIR PUTIN. When I saw PUTIN's face on TV in 1999, I immediately recognized him as the same KGB agent that I talked to, and who said his friend was the admiral in charge of the BLACK SEA FLEET. At the time of PRESIDENT YELTSIN's visit to Vancouver for the Summit Conference, PUTIN, who had supposedly resigned from the KGB, began a political career in St. PETERSBURG. It is quite common for the Head of State (YELTSIN) to take other so called diplomats (PUTIN) when they visit foreign countries. PUTIN was the head of the Foreign Service of the KGB prior to his time in St. PETERSBURG's municipal government. PUTIN first became the prime minister of Russia, a post he held I believe for about four years. Eventually YELTSIN had his battles with his health and political problems and was replaced by PUTIN. PUTIN then had his pick for a prime minister in the name of MEDVEDEV. ONCE YOU ARE A KGB AGENT, YOU ARE ALWAYS A KGB AGENT. So goes the RUSSIAN politics, and the rest is history.

Chapter 46

MY FINAL DAYS IN THE RCMP

In 1994, Her Majesty, The Queen of the British Commonwealth was coming to Victoria and Vancouver. Our VIP section again was tasked with arranging all the necessary security for her visit. All the police personnel were told that all their vacation plans during the scheduled visit would be denied. I was advised by my boss, Sgt. Bruce MONTGOMERY, that because I did such a good job for the CLINTON/YELTSIN Summit Conference, that the RCMP management wanted me to do the same for the queen's visit. I had previously expressed my feelings to various RCMP members that I was considering retiring from the force, having around twenty-five years of service.

Caroline and I had made prior plans for a vacation to California to meet with Caroline's cousin, Yvonne and her husband, Haro BEDALIAN. Haro was the CEO, of BALFOUR BEATTY, a large engineering construction company from the UK, with branches in various countries. I advised Bruce that we had made prior vacation plans and I was going to go to California. He said that our senior boss at the time, Inspector Rick McPHEE advised him that

I must comply with the Senior Management Directive, that all police personnel's vacation plans would be denied. I told Bruce, to tell MCPHEE that I was going, and that was it.

MCPHEE advised Bruce that I must retire immediately. I told Bruce that I would retire when I wanted, and will not adhere to MCPHEE's order, and he should inform MCPHEE of my intentions. Apparently, MCPHEE then met with our division commander Deputy Commissioner Don WILSON, who informed MCPHEE to tell me I could go on my vacation, and I could retire when I wanted. WILSON knew of my dissatisfaction with the force's policy which sidelined my recent promotion opportunity, and that I'd given it my all for the service of this country. It was unnecessary to kick me around much longer. Bruce later told me that D/Commissioner WILSON'S words to MCPHEE were "if Merv wants to go on a holiday, Merv goes on a holiday, I owe him that." I went on my vacation.

The following year, 1995 was my final year in the RCMP. I set the retirement date for April 4, 1995, twenty-five years, two months, and two days since the date of my engagement. Sometime after my anniversary date February 2, I was to be presented with my twenty-five year service ribbon and clasp. The RCMP usually held a big event in the auditorium where a lot of members got their service medals and other awards, and the commanding officer or designate did the presentations. As I was leaving before that date, that duty was handed down to our boss, Inspector Rick MCPHEE. I did not get along with him, but he was to present me with my twenty-five year clasp and ribbon. Sgt. Bruce MONTGOMERY said that Rick wanted me to come to his office where he could do the presentation. I could no longer tolerate the inspector, so I told Bruce that he could send it through the mail, otherwise Bruce could present me with the award.

Bruce said that the inspector was not going to like that, but he told him anyway. The inspector was faced with a dilemma. The senior management would look down on the inspector, as I had a good working relationship with them, but not with the inspector. Well, the inspector came to our office coffee room. Bruce and I met him there, and the inspector presented me with the award. He offered to buy me a coffee. I told him that I did not drink coffee, instead he bought me a 7Up. We had a very brief uncomfortable conversation, and then it ended. I stood up and said, "Thanks", and walked back to my office.

I wanted to slip away unnoticed, but Bruce said that because I'd spent a number of years in a number of different sections within the RCMP, and had contact with a lot of personnel, he felt that we should have a retirement luncheon where several of the members could attend. It was my call, so I said I just wanted our immediate office personnel to attend, as I was not the "big flash kind of guy". That is the way it ended, without the inspector attending.

Unfortunately, Bruce, who was about my age, and had approximately two more months of service than me, and who was very nice guy, had some health problems. He was a diabetic and was overweight. I heard he lost his sight and had to retire. He died a short time later.

Chapter 47

RAPE AND MURDER OF
A FAMILY FRIEND

After Caroline and I were married, Caroline who is of Armenian heritage, met an Armenian woman named Rita at a local exercise club. She struck up a friendship with Rita that continues to this day. Rita and her husband, Yurik MIRZAYAN were originally from Iran, where Yurik served as a major in the SHAH OF IRAN'S ARMY. Prior to the Iranian Revolution in 1979, Rita, Yurik and their two daughters immigrated to the USA. They settled in the Glendale, California area where a lot of the Armenians from Iran left the craziness of the brutal regime of the Revolutionary Guard and set up their homes and businesses. Rita and Yurik eventually decided to immigrate to Canada and settled near where we live. We have had many dinners together and have visited each other on numerous occasions.

On a couple of occasions, we invited Rita, Yurik and their daughter, Christine, who was visiting her parents at the time, to our place for dinner. Christine was such a joy to have around. She had this angelic face and was always smiling and laughing. She was a very intelligent person and I had great, enlightening conversations with her on those occasions.

Christine had just completed her studies at the California University and received her degrees in the faculty of sciences. She had just married a young man who was also in the same academic field. Because of her credentials, intelligence, research, etc., she was offered a position as an Intern at the National Academy Of Sciences in Washington DC. She had only been married a few months when she accepted this position and moved to Washington DC. Her husband was going to join her at a later date and continued living in California.

On the evening of August 1, 1998, Christine having spent a wonderful time at a barbecue with some of her university friends, decided to walk back to her residence along the Potomac River. Along this path, and in the darkness, she was accosted by a Black man and dragged into the nearby bushes. She was brutally raped. Her attacker then smashed her head with a rock several times. Christine's life ended. Then began the mystery of who was her attacker and why?????

On that same day, Rita and Caroline were visiting garage sales in West Vancouver. Rita had purchased a piece of wooden art that they were not able to put into their car, so I was to pick it up the following day in my pickup truck. Rita always received a call from Christine on regular basis and was wondering why Christine had not called her. Rita made some enquires and what came next was the most shocking and the worse emotional fears a parent could hear.

Christine's body was discovered by other people walking along the same pathway that she took that horrific evening. The Washington DC police department did their usual murder investigation and thank GOD that they collected DNA samples. During my time in the RCMP, I had several conversations with other USA police personnel, and at that time, the Washington DC Police Department did not have a very good record in solving crime. Police departments in the USA are administrated differently than in Canada. Funding and administration are handled differently than what I was used to while in the RCMP. What the news media put out across the airwaves was another of the many murders in Washington DC of several young women. One piece of information that was presented to the MIRZAYAN family was that someone who was driving along next to the pathway had witnessed Christine walking and that a Black man was following her.

Christine's body was shipped to West Vancouver. Christine's very distraught parents had to deal with the funeral arrangements. Caroline and I volunteered to help them. We took them to the Capilano View Cemetery Office, where they were to pick out a burial plot. When they found a suitable plot, I, being a spiritualist, suggested to Caroline, that we purchase the two (2) plots next to Christine's. The Capilano View Cemetery do allow room for (2) cremated remains that can be buried on same plot. So, this provided a bit of comfort/connection to the afterlife for Rita and Yurik when their time comes to leave this earth. Caroline and I felt the same way, as we will have four burial spots for our family 's cremated ashes, free of charge. It is expensive to get buried at the present time, especially, in West Vancouver.

Caroline and I assisted Rita and Yurik with a reception after the burial. We had a few of Christine's university colleagues stay at our house, and it was very enlightening to have a conversation with these intellects. I gave the eulogy on behalf of Christine's family. Her older sister, Caroline was living in Denmark, and was not able to attend. In all, it was quite an emotional time for everyone. I did have a long conversation with the president of the National Academy of Sciences from Washington DC, who came to West Vancouver for the funeral services. He was looking for answers surrounding this murder. I did my best to offer him my knowledge on what I hoped the Washington DC police department would have done regarding interviews of likely suspects, and the collection of DNA samples, as once Christine's body is buried, she should not be disturbed. I also told him that perhaps he should contact the FBI and have them involved in this case as there had been a number of murders and sexual assaults, so they must have a serial killer/murderer in their area.

I often visit the Capilano View Cemetery grave sites, and say my prayers to the following:

(1) my former partner, a RCMP member, who committed suicide and is buried at the cemetery, (2) my mother-in-law, ROSALINE, and (3) Christine. I prayed that her murderer would eventually be arrested and hopefully suffer a torturous death.

On November 14, 2019, Rita and Yurik received information that Christine's murderer, GILES DANIEL WARRICK, sixty years old had been arrested in Conway, South Carolina. He was suspected in ten sexual attacks in the Washington DC area. Forensic DNA analysis linked WARRICK to these crimes. I strongly suspect that there are other murders that he is responsible for. Hopefully swift justice will be served in Christine's murder case.

UPDATE: On November 20, 2022, Rita's daughter, Caroline who lives in Denmark received a call from the Washington DC Police Department informing her that WARRICK hung himself in his prison cell. Justice was finally served.

Chapter 48

VACATIONS TO UK, TIBET, CHINA, JAPAN, CAMBODIA, THAILAND, BURMA, NEPAL, INDIA, KENYA, ISRAEL, CUBA

We made several trips to London, UK to visit Caroline's relatives. On one of these trips, Haro was showing me around his London office. I should also mention that Haro had a distinguished honour of having a meeting with Queen Elizabeth II and was a recipient of the OBE for his roadway projects around the United Kingdom. I noticed what appeared to me that there was a very important person coming to visit this office as there were security people present. I asked Haro if he knew what was going on as he was the CEO/ president of this huge company, so he ought to know that someone of importance was coming to his office building. We enquired with a few of the people in the office and they did not know either. All of a sudden, a couple of cars arrived at the front entrance and some men exited these cars and started to come up the stairs. I stood to one side against a wall, while Haro stood across from me. I recognized the important person as being UK MP Jack STRAW, coming up the stairs. He walked up to me and had smile on his face and shook my hand and then walked into one of the meeting rooms. We made some further enquiries and found out that Mr. STRAW was to give a brief speech to a few people in the room. I told Haro that he was the other important person here and Mr. STRAW should have shaken his hand instead of shaking my hand. We had a little laugh and Haro said that Mr. STRAW may have felt that I was someone of importance.

After my retirement, Caroline and I went on various exotic trips around the world. I found trips to the European nations, and other developed nations filled with a lot of history, etc. The ones that were the most eye opening were the Third-World countries, one being Myanmar, formerly known as Burma, which takes you back in time to about 150 years. You see the ox carts, and very primitive living conditions. The people were very humble and friendly.

Tibet, which is occupied by China is another interesting country. It is desolate and barren. With its high attitude, nothing grows above a certain level. Yet the Tibetan people scratch out a living, and are very humble, and polite when you meet them. They are very open to show you their living quarters and are most hospitable. The Tibetan people are of the Buddhist faith. They display their prayer flags, and prayer wheels at various places. China is doing everything to destroy the Tibetan way of living. Some Tibetans have put up a resistance to this occupation, but China with its overwhelming Communist regime has over-populated Tibet and has pretty much conquered this territory. We had an organized tour of China and we did walk on the historical Great Wall which was one of the high lights of this trip.

We visited Nara and Kyoto, Japan, en route to our tour to Thailand, Cambodia, and Burma. Japan is very organized and clean. Houses are very quaint, and people are very polite. Japan is very populated; however, we did not encounter the horror stories of other tourists, who had fought through crowds of people. We got to see some of the ancient shrines. Nara was Japan's original capital before they moved it to Tokyo, one of the most populated cities in the world.

When we inquired about seeing a "GEISHA GIRL," the Japanese people that we talked to found us humorous, and said it was almost impossible, as they were seldom seen in public. So, our tour group was disappointed, and put it off that we would not see one. Four of us went off to have some dinner, which was of small portions, and pretty pricey. We finished our dinner, and were walking back to our hotel, when we spotted a GEISHA GIRL in her kimono walking quite fast on the opposite side of the street. I quickly ran to her, and, in her politeness, she stopped, and I was able to get my friends to take a picture of her and me together. I am sure she realized that we were tourists and wanted to see a GEISHA GIRL. After all she was one of the symbols of Japan.

We continued to travel to Bangkok, Thailand which is an experience. They had a lot of young girls on the streets soliciting, etc. It is a surprisingly, modern city with bright lights, and bustling crowds of people.

Cambodia offered another historical experience with a tour of Angkor Wat, an ancient shrine of sorts. We decided not to go for a tour of the "killing fields." It was where a notorious military leader, Pol Pot, took a lot of intellectuals, and people who opposed him, and marched them into the jungle area, and made them do various sorts of hard labour. He did not feed them much food, etc. Some were tortured in various ways. There are supposedly human skeletons everywhere as you walk around in that area.

A visit to Kenya was amazing. We took in a number of safaris and saw the wild animals in their natural free-range habitat. A lot of this was arranged by Caroline's cousin, Yvonne's daughter, Claire who worked for the United Nations. Some interesting sightings were when the lions were mating and having their meal. They were gorging themselves on a big wild buffalo. The rangers assured us that this animal had been killed by the lions. I believe that this animal was conveniently shot by the rangers, so that the tour guides have the lions available for the tourists to see them eating away and mating whenever the opportunity presented itself. We saw a lot of buffalo herds in this country, and if you came close to the herd, the big bulls with their big menacing horns would come out front, and centre to show their protectiveness of their herd. They are quite capable of killing a lion by using their big menacing horns.

The India trip came a few years later, which coincided with Caroline's school reunion. We arrived in New Delhi, and travelled mostly throughout India by car, driven by an Indian driver. If you were to witness the Indians driving, I highly recommend an Indian driver. The air quality is very polluted, and breathing can be difficult. Toxic fumes are emitted into their environment by their automotive transportation which run mostly on diesel. You would see a lot of spitting, and hacking going on. So quite often the driver would open his vehicle's window and let off a projectile into a vehicle parked next to him in a very crowded, unorganized roadways. There is no argument over this sort of behaviour, as it is quite acceptable.

We spent a few days in Calcutta, where Caroline was born. I must say it was quite an experience. The electric lights would go off unexpectedly, which happens quite frequently there. There are millions of people in this very crowded, ancient, rundown city, with their huge poverty, and pollution, very present as you walk around. There were several aggressive demonstrators / protesters with their placards walking around whom we happened to come upon. I immediately thought of the violent riots that we sometime view on our televisions back home, and the police swinging their sticks beating on the demonstrators. We quickly got out of the area.

India worships a sacred animal "the cow". The cow is allowed to walk, and eat, and do their business freely around India. Coming from a farm in Saskatchewan, l know about cow manure, so we had to be very careful where we stepped. Early one morning while we were in Varanasi to see their morning religious ritual (cremation / burning of human bodies, etc.), we were walking down a narrow dark path, and walked right into a cow. Luckily, we didn't step into a cow pie.

Then came our departure to travel from Calcutta by train to Darjeeling which was a quite an experience. We were staying at one of their upscale rooming houses with a young male attendant, who slept outside our door. He stood guard while we slept and cooked our meals. He also got us our car, and driver. He was a very pleasant, polite fellow, and was always smiling. The ceiling fan worked whenever the power came on. Most of the time it did not work, so it was very uncomfortably hot in the room. In the morning, I went into the bathroom to have a shower and found a dead lizard, or gecko on the floor. I discarded it as Caroline would have freaked out.

We were then driven to Jalda Station by our driver. He told us he would negotiate with a couple of porters to carry our luggage to the train car. There was a huge crowd of people that were looking at us, which to me appeared to be quite frightening. I envisioned them robbing us or stealing our luggage. We started to follow our porters who walked through this crowd quite forcibly. We, being polite Canadians were lagging back a bit. Then I realized that we were going to lose sight of our porters, so I grabbed Caroline, and dragged her as fast as I could to keep us together. I unfortunately shoved a few people aside as they tried to split us up. It was one of the most frightening experiences, ever.

We found our train car, which had four bunk beds in it. The porters were kind to store our luggage in the car. I paid them, and off they went. I checked the roster posted outside the car, and we were to share these quarters with an Indian Army general, and a civilian named Mr. Singh. Caroline immediately got upset and said that we were to get a private car to ourselves. I said that this is India with a large population, and they need to use every available space. We should be lucky that we got through that menacing crowd. I told Caroline to take one of the top bunks, and I would take the one below hers.

Within a few minutes we had a couple of Indian soldiers come into the train car carrying their rifles. They checked the quarters out, and said the general was coming soon. A short time later, the general and Mr. Singh arrived. We introduced ourselves. Mr. Singh took the other top bunk, and the general took the bottom bunk. They were both friendly. Mr. Singh immediately removed his turban, and wrapped his long hair into another turban, and went to sleep. Caroline was also a bit tired and went to sleep in her bunk bed. The general was joined by his colonel, and the three of us had a wonderful conversation on world affairs, etc. I then told them that I had had an exhausting day, and excused myself, and went to sleep.

During the night Caroline woke me up, and said she had to go the toilet. We walked out of our car, and down to another a car further down that housed the toilet. This toilet was a hole in the floor, and you had to straddle it to do your business while the train was rocking around on the train tracks. I had to hold onto Caroline, so she didn't fall in. It was a laughable experience.

Caroline got sick on the train trip from Calcutta Jalda train station to Darjeeling. Darjeeling is where she attended her primary school back in the 1950's. So, I attended her reunion by myself, and met some of her friends, and gave them the sad news of Caroline's illness. Darjeeling is located in the foothills of the Himalayan mountains and is spectacular to see. The first man to climb Mt Everest was a Tibetan named Tenzing Norquay, who lived in Darjeeling. Caroline said that she, and her friends used to go to his horse-riding station and had met Tenzing when she was going to school in Darjeeling.

India is a country that works with its various levels of government from a socialist ideology, to what we in the west know as a democracy. It has a very large distinct rich Hindu culture, with every other religion in the world amongst its population. It is the second most populous country in the world, and the largest democratic country in the world. It has its poverty with homeless people living right outside, next to the homes of some of the wealthy property owners. They all carry on with their lives. It is worth a visit for those who are able to stomach poverty, illness, and yet see the historical culture of the country.

In my retirement, I met through friends of ours, a former jet fighter pilot, Yadi SHARIFIRAD from the Iranian Air Force, who flew many sorties during the Iran/Iraq war. He was arrested by his government 's (Iranian) secret police, and tortured for being a so called "SPY" and connected to the American CIA. He was eventually released from prison, and escaped to Turkey, through the Orient countries, and eventually ended up living in Vancouver. He wrote a book about his ordeal called *The Flight Of The Patriot*, which is well worth reading.

The trip to Cuba was an eyeopener. Being a Communist country there were security guards everywhere. The people are very humble and friendly. We had a buffet dinner with limited variety at our resort, which served what they said was stewed chicken. However, I suspected it was alligator, which they have in abundance. We had a tour around the island, one being the Bay of Pigs. This is where the Cubans fought with the American forces, and the rise of Fidel CASTRO. It was also amazing to see the old 1950's and the odd early 1960's American cars rumbling along on their streets. Some were haphazardly patched up, others somewhat restored to their original state.

Chapter 49

MY FRIEND ANDRE

In my retirement and having attended a number of cocktail parties with friends, I met a man named "Andre ", who had an interesting background. In our conversations, he said that when he was a young boy growing up in Poland, he could remember his country occupied by the Nazis during the Second World War. He was on a train with his mother and young brother on their way to the Auschwitz concentration camp. He did not know what was happening at the time, other that they were forced onto the train with a lot of other people. The train came to a station-stop somewhere before Auschwitz. There were soldiers with guns all around the train. He, together with his mother and young brother were told to get off the train, which they did. They stood on the station platform while the train proceeded to Auschwitz.

Apparently, his uncle, who had some nobility status in Poland had bribed the Nazi regime in getting them off the train, thus saving them from the horrific outcome that we all read about in history books, documents, etc.

Andre said that not only had he dealt with the Nazi regime, but the Communist regime that came after the war. It was a dismal life, and he was very unhappy, so he decided to escape.

Andre had managed to get onto a cargo ship going to the United Kingdom. There he found some employment working in a bar, serving drinks. He said that all the generous patrons would leave him tips by telling him to buy himself a drink. He took their money and put it away for his living expenses and did not buy himself a drink. He managed to save enough money over a period of time and immigrated to Canada. He got a job showing apartment suites for a building developer whose family came from Poland. He was a pretty good artist and managed to sell some of his paintings.

Unfortunately, Andre had some health problems. He did not elaborate on what they were, but when he was at our house during one of our parties, he sat to the side away from other people who were mingling around on our back patio. I was busy with all the quests and did not spend much time with him at the time. When the food was served, the other quests took the food and sat down in various places inside our house. I was outside with few of the guests. Eventually I picked up some food and joined Andre, who was sitting by himself by one of our picnic tables. We had a conversation. He was having a very difficult time breathing. He was a private man, so I never questioned about his breathing. It was a short time later that I learned that his condition got worse. I went to see him and his wife, Jacqueline at their condo in Vancouver. It was a very, very sad visit. He died shortly after my visit on July 2, 2017. I later learned from a doctor friend of ours, that it was the worst kind of death, because you eventually cannot breathe and you die choking to death. I think of him often as I do of other friends who have passed away a way too soon. So far GOD has looked after me, but for how long, HE HAS NOT TOLD ME.

Chapter 50

AWARD PRESENTATION

After a series of several calls from S/S/M John BUIS and C/Supt Deanne BURLEIGH from the Burnaby detachment, John felt that Jack Robinson and I should get some recognition for saving his and Jack's life in this gunfight that we were involved on April 22, 1979.

The date was finally set for May 20, 2021, and the award presentation would be held at the RCMP Headquarters, 14200 Green Timbers Way, Surrey, B.C., and Deputy Commissioner Jennifer STRACHAN wanted to make the presentation. Jack and I were to wear our Red Serge uniforms, etc. I got my uniform out of the closet and tried it on. To my surprise and not unexpected, my pants needed to be let out as my waistline had increased a few inches. I managed to get the high brown boots to fit OK. Now I had to get my uniform altered. I went to a local tailor to get my pants let out.

The woman about my age was most willing to do the alterations with quick short notice. She told me to try the uniform pants on. So, I went into a small, restricted cubicle that had grey curtains around it, and a bench to sit down on. I had at my home been able to take my jeans off while balancing on one leg, sometime supporting myself against a wall. Well, I thought I should be able to do that in this small cubicle. I ignored sitting down on the bench. I proceeded to remove my jeans. Low and behold, it was my BIG MISTAKE. I managed to get one pant leg off, then lost my balance and came crashing through these grey curtains landing on my rear end and flat on my back coming to a sudden stop when I hit the concrete floor. I immediately got a back muscle spasm. I could barely move. There I was with one pant leg off, in my underwear and not able to get to remove the jeans from the other leg. The female tailor came to my rescue. I managed to curl up and tried to stretch my back muscles. She asked if I was OK. I said I was OK and more embarrassed about the whole thing and started to laugh. She did help me get up onto the bench. With a lot of back pain, I got dressed up in my uniform pants and the tailor took the measurements.

I went home in a lot of pain and did a lot explaining to everyone who inquired as to why I was moving very slowly. I tried to humour everyone and told them to laugh, because this was laughable from my point of view.

On MAY 20, I had Vanessa my youngest stepdaughter, to drive me to the Surrey RCMP HQ. We had a few laughs about my uniform adjustments. Photos were taken of the Award Presentation.

I had a very brief conversation with Deputy Commissioner Jennifer STRACHAN and told her that this was not the first time I had been shot at. I briefly told her of that incident back in 1971 in Gibson's, when she was just a very young girl growing up. She said something to the effect of me having nine lives. I had a laugh at it. The Burnaby gunfight was a very intense thirty-to-fifty-five second gunfight, something you would see in the American Western movie gunfights, like Wyatt EARP, or in the movie episodes of the UNTOUCHABLES with Eliot NESS. Perhaps in my previous spiritual life I was within Wyatt EARP's group in the Wild West America, or Eliot NESS's group dealing with all the bad guys and the bootlegging in the 1920's and 1930's. We had one thing in common, WE WERE LAWMEN.

Having time to reflect on this award presentation, I wanted to thank D/Commissioner STRACHAN again and what effect it had on my stepdaughter's appreciation with all the ceremonial stuff, etc. I left a few phone messages on the D/Commissioner voice mail. Her assistant called me back, saying the D/Comm would call me back around 13:00 hrs on Tuesday, June 8.

At 13:03, I received a call from D/Commissioner STRACHAN. I told her that she was the second D/Comm to call me in my career. The previous call was from D/Comm Don WILSON, back in 1990's telling me, that he was disappointed that he could not get me promoted from a corporal to sergeant, in the position of being in charge, of our media liaison. It was a job that I was doing for about a year, and had the full support of my boss, (Supt. L. HENSCHEL) at the time. As a matter of fact, I wrote up the job requirements for the media liaison section. However, our RCMP Headquarters in Ottawa, had changed the staffing rules, procedures, etc. D/Commissioner WILSON told me that he was able to override Ottawa's decision in the past, but now was advised that Ottawa HQ dictated the promotional procedures. I told him that I was most disappointed in being back stabbed again by the RCMP and would consider early retirement. He said he understood my position.

Looking back at my life, and with all the turmoil, violence, and ethnic wars going on in various countries around the world, I think that we should all strive to being a good citizens and try to get along with all other human beings and help one another if, and when it is possible. Unfortunately, that is impossible, only wishful thinking. Perhaps the politicians should take a breather, and listen to words of John LENNON'S song, "IMAGINE".

On April 22, 2022, on a pleasant sunny afternoon, retired Staff Sergeant Major John BUIS, retired Staff Sergeant Jack ROBINSON, Chief Superintendent Graham de la GORGENDIERE, OIC of the Burnaby detachment and I met for lunch at a Burnaby restaurant. This date was significant as it was forty-three years earlier that I'd shot Gustave John Steve GYULAY, (see Chapter 27). After lunch we all met in front of the Fountain Tire Store, formerly the Good Year Tire Store for a group photo, where the actual shooting took place. I am sure for BUIS and ROBINSON there were some emotional feelings about being shot there forty-three years earlier. Thank God that I was calm throughout this gunfight and my first bullet struck GYULAY'S chest area and continued into his liver which slowed him down, otherwise he would have come around the Lincoln. and shot Jack with his second shotgun blast. Shooting with a .38 cal revolver at a moving target in the early evening, with darkness settling in was a challenge. I, in my spiritual sense, could only say that God looked after me that evening, as HE has done that so many times in my crazy, eventful life. I jokingly say to some of my friends that every time I get to the PEARLY GATES IN HEAVEN, I MEET UP WITH GOD AND HE TELLS ME THAT HE HAS ANOTHER JOB FOR ME AND WITH LIGHTNING SPEED I AM SENT BACK DOWN TO EARTH, AND I AM STILL HERE, CARRYING ON.

In my conclusion, I will make one statement, WISE PEOPLE MAKE WISE DECISIONS, STUPID PEOPLE MAKE STUPID DECISIONS. Somewhere in between there is a lot of chaos and happiness, which makes this world we live in interesting. In my previous job in the RCMP, I encountered quite a few stupid people and was instrumental in getting them put in the "crowbar hotel".

As I finish writing this story, the war is going on in Ukraine with PUTIN's horrific, murderous campaign to destroy Ukraine and is committing genocide. I believe PUTIN has a huge ego and wants to be "THE TSAR," who brought all the former countries that were part of the Soviet Union into his empire. In these modern times, he is the most inhumane, barbaric, murderous leader of a notorious country of this world (and there are others) to the brink of World War III.

So, my story ends. If you have some comments, good or bad, I would appreciate an email from you at Mkorolek47@gmail.com

CPSIA information can be obtained
at www.ICGtesting.com
Printed in the USA
LVHW010403100623
749400LV00006B/17